SCARLET LETTER #3

The Wild and the Free:
Shane, Rousseau, Hippies

by
Donal McGraith

Canadian Cataloguing in Publication Data
McGraith, Donal
The Wild and The Free: Shane, Rousseau, Hippies
978-1-895166-32-3
1. Cultural Theory. I. Title.

Printed and bound in North America.

First published 2014
Ⓝ
No Copyright

Published by Charivari
1 Coin St. #607,
Etobicoke, ON M8V 3Y9
Canada

Cover photograph by Nickolas Muray, public domain

A doctor of nothing, I firmly kept myself apart from all semblance of participation in circles that then passed for intellectual or artistic. I admit that my merit in this respect was well tempered by my great laziness, as well as by my very meagre capacities for confronting the work of such careers. Never to have given more than a very slight attention to questions of money, and absolutely none to the ambition of holding some brilliant post in society...

—Guy Debord

Preface

This book is on the one hand deeply pessimistic, while on the other hand it is wildly optimistic. On both counts it may be considered crackpot, and not only because it cannot be falsified and therefore is in no way scientific. As for the pessimism, I think we all know that things are very bad. We have seen and are experiencing the early effects of climate change, and yet there are pundits everywhere who continue to deny this. I am sure that many people, if not most, doubt the sincerity of this convenient position. Given the current character of debate, where people with pessimistic views are merely shouted down as doom sayers, and research is severely compromised by corporate involvement in the funding of research and universities, the media pundits are able to spread confusion mixed with fear. And most people just have to get on with their lives, so making any significant change is unlikely. They may want ecological solutions to transit and food but such solutions are difficult to find, expensive and sometimes dubious or misguided.

The current life world is driven by consumerism. Jobs depend on it as do lifestyles. The inevitability of waste and pollution are soul-crushing. Those that profit from creating a disposable consumerism promulgate it through the culture they pay for, which defines a humanity predisposed to a throwaway culture. Some parts are simple; we must work hard and do things we don't want to do to get by. We are told we are by nature acquisitive and feel that happiness resides in things, in particular, consumerism. The things we have now, afford us a better life than humanity has ever experienced. We in the developed economies are instructed that we are far better off, with more fulfilling lives now than humanity has ever known. And further, we will eventually bring this happy lifestyle to the rest of the world.

And here is where this book flips to being wildly optimistic and is likely hard to believe. I posit that there was a time when we were much happier and it lasted for a very long time. I also posit that we all know this, but have a hard time figuring out how we can have it. Some of us think that substantial wealth will bring it to us. While that might free us from some of the anxieties of modern life, it only brings other anxieties.

And yet I think you know that this other kind life is possible.

Introduction

About 25 years ago I started to joke with my friends that all movies were *Shane*. It's pure hyperbole of course, but there was a solid point behind it. *Shane* encapsulates many of the most important themes in cinema. These themes are central to Western literature as well. One can probably point at any classic text or movie, Homer's *Odyssey* or *Richard III*, and see many similar connecting themes. While I am sure there are many stories that share important characteristics with it, *Shane*, at least for me, has a mother lode of common but interesting themes (and its own peculiarities).

Shane is not the main point of this book, only its starting point. Released in 1953, just prior to the dominance of television and a new wave of rapid changes in media technology, it is a popular example of modernism that returns to a mythic past in order to illuminate the future. The movie embodies old ideals at the brink of rapid suburbanization which destroys any possibility of a rural life, let alone the wandering self-sufficiency of the outlaw Shane, or the totally male world of lawless wide open spaces represented by the cattlemen, or the dignity of the hunter-gatherer Native people, or even the folksy communitarian ideals of the homesteaders. While vestiges of rural life still existed for awhile, by the time Shane arrived in the theatre it was for all intents and purposes dead. The Western was a dominant film theme of my childhood when my own transition as a small child from city to suburbia reflected the end of another relic, the homestead farming of *Shane*. Farming surrounded the suburban town that I grew up in for miles and miles and that town now has swallowed it all. When I came to town like the little boy in *Shane*, the farmer boys in my school were like Shane and the outlaw Wilson, already relics, and they instinctively hated us. Levittown is the monster that ate the family farm.

The Western movie as a cinematic prototype is represented here by *Shane*. Others could do just as well, but *Shane* was the one that for me inspired this meditation. Westerns are archetypal stories that draw from the *Iliad* or the *Odyssey*. *Shane* is not a 'classic' Western as many before me have pointed out. Shane represents something of a break in Westerns. Shane is an anti-hero, and after *Shane* anti-heroes start to figure more prominently in the Western. *Shane*, by breaking with expectations, throws into relief important elements of the Western.

I was born about a year after the movie was released. The movie was already a harbinger of things to come in my life as a baby boomer. The first flat wide screen film, a format invented to compete with television, something TV couldn't do for nearly half a century. Though it was originally released with an optical sound track, it was, after its initial success, re-mixed on a three track stereophonic sound track.

I grew up in a family mad for movies. From the time I was old enough to go, my family would see at least a movie a week and in the summer often 2 or even 3 at the drive-ins. We watched movies on TV all the time and I watched on my own. Probably around age 6 or 7 I was a big James Cagney fan and used to do imitations of him and Jimmy Durante. My great aunt, who I spent several summers with, let me stay up to watch *Starlight Theatre* on CBC to complete my cinematic education, particularly of film noir.

Shane draws from film noir which itself drew from Westerns, and shares similar themes. *Shane* is an early example of a Western that puts noir elements in stark relief. That overpowering hot sun in *Shane*, the unremitting light that fills key scenes, cast more ominous shadows than many film noir movies. There are night scenes and mud-filled grey scenes as well. It is not really hardboiled like classic noir, but the film is significantly without hope. Despite the big sky, it is more claustrophobic than the typical noir film's grimy tenements and alleyways.

I first saw *Shane* in high school, well after I was already familiar with *Murder Incorporated* and *The Big Sleep*. *Shane* was shown in the school's large auditorium for most if not the whole school. I don't remember why. I was not all that impressed at the time. But the images and story of the movie were permanently stored in my visual memory. And for some reason, many years later I could recall most of the movie from memory.

What interests me about *Shane* is not so much its qualities as a movie, but as a vehicle to get to important themes in Western culture which have a bearing on my own ideas in philosophy, politics and ethics. It is a good story to frame certain arguments on that I keep coming back to: Loyalty vs. Integrity; Love vs. Violence; Intentions vs. Consequences; Law vs. Rough Justice; Male Sexuality vs. The Family; Nomads vs. Civilization; Gangs; and recently for me, Rousseau, most importantly his *Essay Concerning the Origin of Inequality.*

As a child of the sixties I was of course immersed in the whole of 60s popular culture not just the movies. The counter-culture and its commodification were my daily reality. So the themes of the 60s youth movements such as anti-racism, anti-war, alternative economies, hippies, back to the land, ecology, and feminism were absorbed easily from popular culture, but I was also the type to dig further. And so I read widely and considered the theories and ideology of the 60s and like so many others found its roots in earlier thinkers of the 20th century and beyond, back centuries into the early development of the modern. So I followed the links in popular culture to Jung, Freud, Marcuse, Camus, Sartre, Marx and so on. Eventually after pursuing interests academically I dropped out of a PhD in philosophy, a degree that guaranteed a career driving cab. I then spent 7 years in a lefty bookstore run as a workers collective. This all ended in the mid-80s along with that last self-destructive gasp of internecine theory that brought us identity politics. Our politics became so microscopically designed that the new right waltzed in and swept those not in the academy into smaller more irrelevant corners. And those in the academy were more worried about tenure than politics, their leftist stance more of a wine and book club thing than any kind of activism.

Ah yes, post-modernism, thirty years of logorrhea followed, reaching its pinnacle in the inane vacuous nose-pulling blathering of uber-Stalinist hack Slavoj Žižek. The essential prerequisite for academic success in the PoMo world is tortured syntax, lots of self-referential terminology, quoting endlessly and saying nothing that can be pinned down. There is no more disheartening sight than that found on Youtube: Slavoj Žižek at OWS (i.e. Occupy Wall Street). Here Žižek instructs the Occupy movement about the meaning of what they are doing. He reads his text which they dutifully repeat. Well, they are probably mostly post-graduate students so they are trained to repeat what they are told. Does anyone ever get up in Žižek's classes and tell him that he 'works for the man!'?

And so, in the reflections that follow, I begin with an analysis of *Shane* but do so because it is an effective way into a discussion of my abiding concerns regarding ethical integrity and autonomy, those longings which we all viscerally feel for the wild and the free.

On *Shane*

"The Greatest Story of the West Ever Filmed."
"A mysterious stranger rode in from out of nowhere to play a decisive role
in the lives of these rugged pioneers. 'Call me Shane.' Shane who attracted
the woman with his quiet strength. Who fascinated the boy with the glint
of his gun. ...From the clash of elemental forces, George Stevens has created
a motion picture unforgettable for its spectacle and scope; its great human
story; its deadly conflict;
I've heard about you.
What've you heard Shane?
I've heard that you're a low down Yankee liar. ...
There never was a man like Shane."[1]

A man on a horse wanders through a valley in Wyoming sometime after the
Homestead Act of 1862. A rough plain, set against mountains, stretches
out for miles. A river runs through it. A deer stands and watches. The sun
is bright and hard. The scrub and water decorate the movements of the rider and
his horse who walk slowly as though they are the singular lonesome inhabitants.

He comes upon a homestead.
"I hope you don't mind me cutting through your place"
"No, I guess not."
"Headin' north. ... Didn't expect to find any fences around here."[2]

He's looking for work. He's quite handy with a gun. He is worshipped by
the boy, attracts the wife and befriends the father. The way he draws the affections
from each member of this family is not unlike the stranger in Pasolini's *Teorama*.
The cattlemen are fed up with homesteaders putting up fences, so they try
to push them out, run their cattle through their land, intimidate and threaten
them. Shane knows this is trouble but he cannot stand by. Compelled to act, he
and the father put a licking on several of the cattlemen. Infuriated, the cattle boss
(Ryker) hires a gunslinger: Jack Palance (Wilson). The man in black. A caricature
of evil, but evil just the same.[3] Without blinking an eye he guns down a foolish
ex-confederate soldier with too much courage.
At the funeral the homesteaders decide to band together to fight. They
nominate the boy's father as leader. The newcomer Shane picks a fight with the
father to save him from certain death. Shane goes off to kill Wilson (Jack Palance)

1. All text from the official Paramount trailer for *Shane* (Paramount Pictures, 1953).
2. Dialogue quoted from the opening scene of *Shane* (Paramount Pictures).
3. See the final three paragraphs of this section.

13

and he tells him that they are both relics of the Old West, but Wilson hasn't realized it yet. After the gunfight Shane leaves on his horse, wounded, perhaps dying, the boy calls after him, "Shane, come back…"

In the cliché Western, a John Wayne B flick, the cowboy is seduced by the woman to settle down, to leave his wild ways behind. In its most basic form the Western opposes the free-range life of the cowboy to the staid and polite domesticity of settled family life. The cowboy by definition is inimical to domesticity. How he is seduced is a key theme of Westerns but it is also an archetypal theme in Western culture. This story of seduction within conflicting life worlds manifests itself in many ways in Westerns. There are two main conflict narratives within which there is typically a seduction of the hero. One is the conflict between homesteaders and free-range men, the other is the conflict between homesteaders and 'Indians.'

Indians are an alternate kind of free-rangers in Westerns. Indians in Westerns are usually buffalo-hunting plains tribes. In some movies they can parallel or take the place of the dynamic between free-range and family oriented agriculture with its fences and land deeds. In other cases the White cattlemen are fighting Indians for the same massive range area. White free-rangers represent large mammal domestication. Indians, in fact, were even more 'free-range' in their hunter-gatherer subsistence. There are key differences between what free-range means in these competing cultures.

The romanticisation of Native Americans[4] by anthropologists, missionaries and philosophers has tried to fabricate an original Native unity amongst tribes. In fact, prior to as well as after Columbus, there was widespread internecine warfare in North America. Large game hunting tribes fought against other tribes of the same ilk as well as agriculturist tribes should they encroach. Tribes who suffered a loss of food source would attack rival tribes to take land or game. Much of the central dynamic of the Western was already *de rigueur* in America before the White Man.

The Indian's savage life is cited by Rousseau as closest in existence to his idea of life without anxiety, but they are not, despite persistent claims, one and the same states. The ideal form is when a more primitive human has the ability, through purely one's own means, to eke out a living without law, marriage and

---

4. I will be somewhat liberal with the name I gave to those people who were living in the Americas when Europeans came to destroy them by war and disease, or perhaps bring the wonders of European civilization, depending on your point of view. I will on occasion use the absurd term 'Indian' especially when discussing the Western in film and *Shane* because in some sense the absurdity of the term matches the absurdity of the portrayal. I will use 'Native' as well, though indistinct, is at least factual if too general. I may use aboriginal as well because I am not afraid of words, I do not belong to any cult, or indicate membership in any society celebrating colonialism or imperialism through the use of any of these terms. But please, go to town, call me whatever names you like, I know it makes you feel superior and I encourage that.

family. The individual ideal, described in Rousseau, is more like a mountain man, the missing link, where each is responsible primarily for his or her own well-being.

The tribe is quite distinct as it does add family and group obligations. A tribe works together to ensure group survival, so children survive and continue the tribe. But Rousseau saw that in the Native American there was, relative to the European, a degree of self-sufficiency not prevalent in modernity.

In contrast to the Indian, the cattlemen are a pure gang, in that the survival of children is not at issue at all, in fact, this seems completely out of the question. Women and children would just slow them down. So the gang does not reproduce itself, it recruits. Boys chose to leave their family to join the gang. The gang is doomed, but it can hang on by recruiting the wayward. In this, the cattlemen as a gang have one thing in common with Rousseau's 'natural man,' they do not procreate to survive. Free-range Natives are limited by many filial obligations as well as by ritual social obligation.

So while the Indians are not white, and thus considered untrustworthy and devious, they are in this way closer to homesteaders than cattlemen. Native bands have baggage and obligations that they share with the homesteaders. But they are competing for the same land and while there are these similarities, what is more important to the homesteaders is their sense of civilization, their language, culture and religion. European culture demands the eradication of the Native lifestyle far more vigorously than it requires the restraint of cattlemen. European culture has a place for gangs. So while the White cattlemen may represent an unruly idea of the romantic natural man, the outlaw, freedom and unfettered male sexuality, they are ultimately bracketed by the law. They do not truly live outside the law. In the movies, the cattlemen often convey nostalgia for a true outlaw life but they require the law to energize their self-conception. Cattlemen, in the end, trade in the same economy as the homesteaders. They are buying and selling commodities. They do not drive cattle to feed themselves.

This brings to mind other sorts of outlaw gangs in the Western, the kind that rob stagecoaches and banks, and the gunmen. These are, of course, the same criminal activities that take place in the cities back east. It is only a matter of style as to how they differ from their urban counterparts. Of course they do exploit the same space for a form of lawlessness opened up by the cattlemen but also provided to them by the context of small populations in vast rural areas. So it is not surprising to see these outlaws in the Western context standing in for a similar romantic naturalism as that found amongst the cattlemen. This is not unlike the way that film noir characters take on an ersatz existential style.

Gangs and families share many aspects. Sometimes families can operate like gangs. Mafia comes from *ma familia*, my family. There is no surprise here.

Tribes are created by extended families. The Indians, like the Mafia, incorporate a band of brothers within a family structure with domesticity and specific obligations. The Indians maintain an outlet within their structure for the expression of gang-like behaviour in warriors and express their pent up violence, usually against other tribes.

Though in movies the cattlemen often have little context except that they are the bad guys or problematic, obviously, in reality, they are much more like the Mafia, having families as well as being gang members. And as we have seen, there are glimpses of this in many Westerns. The assumption is that prior to the building of an extensive train system, cattle needed to be driven great distances to the nearest abattoir or a cattle train. And so, in this period, cattlemen lived on their own away from family ties, like the military or sailors or lumbermen or any isolated work crew. So they represent a special case that highlights some of the prominent features of gangs. They are, in this situation, more purely a gang, a band of brothers, more peculiarly anti-family and anti-woman, whereas the Indians are not.

In the movies, the historical reality is only a premise for the mythic meaning. In the Western, the cattlemen are archetypes as are the homesteaders and the Indians. The primary conflict is between free-ranging cattlemen and homesteaders. It is a replay in the new U.S. frontier of the original transition and conflict between agriculture and hunter-gatherer societies. The so-called 'open frontier' made this old conflict new again. Early settlers in the East were agriculturists whose main conflict was with Natives who often were agriculturists themselves and so the dispute was over land as the Europeans encroached and drove back Native populations.

In the Wild West there were vast areas of apparently open land. This land existed in territories claimed but not supervised. The particular style of cattle industry arose to meet the opportunity. The territories were wild, beyond the reach of the law. Here the conflict with the Natives paralleled the first conflicts. Just as it was agriculturists versus agriculturists in the east, it was free-ranging cattlemen versus free-ranging hunter-gatherer Natives in the west. The Natives hunt buffalo and that life style meant being mobile over large areas. The cattlemen wanted the same area to drive cattle. They did not want to share or compete with Natives, nor have cattle compete with buffalo for forage. The Natives did not want cattlemen to drive their cattle through buffalo areas.

The conflict between homesteaders and cattlemen mirrored the conflict between homesteaders and Natives. Wherever farms appeared there would be less land for buffalo and less land for Natives. This eventually led to the Indian wars as the U.S. government attempted to bring law to the West. Bringing law and political legitimacy to the territories essentially favoured the homesteaders and heightened the conflict between them and cattlemen as well as the conflict between homesteaders and Natives.

As the war turned in favour of the Whites and the Natives were forced to rear guard actions, the U.S. government at one point wanted to turn Cheyenne and Arapaho into settled agriculturalists. The reservation system was created and then fragmented. Originally the great Sioux reservation was most of South Dakota, perhaps enough to preserve some element of their hunting culture, but under homesteader pressure the large reservation was divided into five smaller units. This effectively destroyed the plains Natives' way of life.

The homesteaders in the Western usually represent the good guys. If the conflict is between cattlemen or soldiers and Indians then whoever is white is generally good. Western movies play out several different class conflict options. Cattlemen and homesteaders may join to fight Indian encroachment, but there will still be a tension between them. That is because homesteaders, as well as representing an encroachment on the range, represent the law, property, family and capital. And in the movies they also represent love. Love versus violence. Family, law, property and capital tag along like parasites to love.

As stated above, the classic Western concludes when the woman gets the man. It is the transition from the man's world to the woman's world, at least insofar as women are constructed in Westerns. Women represent domesticity, sexual love, family love, and educe fatherly love or they are prostitutes. Sometimes in Westerns, cattlemen will have a family superstructure just as in the Mafia movies, but what is paramount with both Mafia and cowboys is the gang structure. Sometimes the band of brothers will be actual brothers and other kin. They will mirror a kind of honour sometimes upheld by Indians. However, whether or not cattlemen have mothers or wives, there will always be a potential for sexual violence and humiliation. Their sense of family is exclusive and outlaw. Disputes are settled by force both inside and outside the family. Women connected to a gang, such as mothers or sisters, must not love outside this structure. The band of brothers is not necessarily patriarchal in the sense of some birthright; it is more about power seized and power maintained by force. It is a doomed social structure: the more powerful you are, the more threatened you become. The gang member is automatically paranoid, and the gang leader lives under a constant threat of violence. The gang, paranoid and anxious, means to survive by spreading paranoia and anxiety.

Variations exist. Some of the homesteaders are converted cattlemen. And there is the converted gunman who becomes a Sheriff or Marshall. This particular sub-genre is like an afterlife for Shane had he chosen to stay. But homesteaders are a suburban plague. They are developers buying up land and turning a profit. The success of some attracts the hopes of others. And so they flood into areas encroaching into the areas that cattlemen and Indians need. They destroy the conditions necessary for a free-range life. And over the period which Western movies were popular, it is no coincidence that it was marked by rapid suburbanization.

The bad guys in *Shane* are hollow and lacking nuance. Earlier in this section I called them caricatures. Depictions of evil are caricatures by necessity because evil is inimical to being human. It is a problem of freedom, where freedom becomes abstract, moving from choices that generally benefit to choices that benefit one over another. The choice of evil is tempting when Satan asks us the question, "Why not?" And because God created Satan and the snake, God knew the inevitable result. So God creates theodicy in the snake. And from this derives the impossibility of ethics a la Kant: our freedom demands pathological acts, evil acts and lies.

The creation story is a nefarious justification of slavery for the purposes of agriculture. Eden is pre-agriculture. After the fall Cain and Abel carry forward the story: "Why not kill rivals?" Rivalry is post palaeolithic; post-self-sufficiency. It is, as in *Shane*, the agriculturist killing the herder. The murder of Abel is weak and pathetic, common attributes of evil. Cain and Abel are not self-sufficient, they are competitors for land and resources. Their dependency is represented by God and religion. The droughts and plagues that are foretold in the early part of the Bible are descriptions of ecological disasters brought on by agriculture and animal husbandry.

The snake in the Garden of Eden is a cartoon distraction from the real evil. Everything in Genesis is backward. In the Garden of Eden, Eve and Adam are frugivores. The do not labour, labour is their punishment. It is a purely nonsensical justification of agriculture and religion. I am not quite sure how anyone can buy the idea the omnipotent creator who knows the future, creates a perfect world and then destroys it through his own agent. And since he knows the result is thousands of years of pain and suffering, what is this god but a sadistic creep with the mind of a child. A child pulling the legs off a grasshopper and enjoying the miserable result.

The Surprise.

The Consummation.

Male Sexuality vs. Family

The cattlemen, the men of the range in the movies are made to reflect a very 'pure' free-range life. It is a life almost entirely without women. Relations with women are intermittent, episodic and quick. Free-rangers are implied rapists, even when this was not made explicit in the movie due to the Hayes code or for marketing reasons. There are movies of this type where rape is more explicitly dealt with but most just imply its occurrence indirectly. To the adult audience it is clear, even if it is not overtly portrayed or named. An ominous inevitability of rape hangs over Westerns.

The other typical way cattlemen relate to women in these movies, either explicitly or implicitly, is as prostitutes. The women who populate the taverns are often not named as prostitutes. This is, though, implicitly understood. So the men of the range either pay or take sex, they do not seduce, or court. They are never looking for marriage because marriage is inimical for a free-ranger. The ideal cattleman is an outlaw. Outlaw, not so much as a criminal under the law, but beyond the law. The range is a space where the law does not apply. In the Western, the outlaw is the ultimate example of raw male sexuality. Married women, good women, are always intimidated by their presence. These men exude a visceral sexuality that is always accompanied by a threat of violence. They are not tender. They are not the marrying kind. In fact they are a threat to all marriage, as rape or prostitution are their only options for a woman. 'Good' women are like wild horses that need to be broken (read shamed). Once tainted by rape they become prostitutes. A story occasionally told by a saloon woman.

Similarly, Indian men in Westerns are also considered potential rapists. This is not because they are savages. Westerns do show a kind of ambivalence of Indian-qua-savage. Movies often show the same Natives as living in families despite being parallel competitors to free-range cattlemen, who are completely anti-family. Kinship rules and appropriate relations between men and women Natives are implied. Rape is rarely implied within a tribe. Though Westerns do not deal with this, like all such social structures, rape was always an accepted form of violence when one attacks rival tribes, and for the Natives, the homesteaders are just another tribe, as are the cattlemen, both of whom threaten the Native way of life.

The cattlemen in Westerns imply a more exclusively male world than the Indians, and also present a violent sexual threat to 'good white women.' The cattlemen are a gang, a band of brothers, a social organization that has continued to exist in all human cultures to the present day. The current gangsta culture in music videos and movies is precisely the same gang culture. Violence is the main currency of the gang. Our current gangs undermine family oriented homesteads, even if in a distinctly urban environment.

In a gang of brothers who practice violent intermittent sexuality there is, as well, a large component of homo-eroticism. It is a not the eroticism that is represented by the repressed gay love scene in a movie such as *Brokeback Mountain*. This homo-eroticism of the Western is more akin to the culture of Genet's *Our Lady of the Flowers*; male on male rape. Most classic Westerns only hint at this but it is a certain result of this wholly male culture. More contemporary prison movies have made this culture explicit. In prison movies it is portrayed correctly as a form of dominance, with, as well, a kind of abusive coupling, an inverted marriage. Male on male rape is also a form for punishment or humiliation. One gang member may rape a member of another gang to throw down a gauntlet or as retribution. This can also happen within the gang itself. Some very low members in a gang may be subject to randomly forced sexuality.

Mutuality is not necessarily excluded. The circle jerk might be a comic aspersion but it is likely not that far from the truth of long isolated all male group-ings. Sometimes a relationship may just fulfill needs but it cannot be allowed to undermine authority, so extreme heterosexual machismo is the only public face of these men. Brutal rape of women is sometimes a necessary antidote to any hint of homosexual taint, as a proof of not being a 'faggot.' Of course there is an irony in this, since rape does, strangely, imply an aversion to and fear of women.

So the sexuality of the cattlemen (the gang) is deeply conflicted. Violence is a deep-seated component of it and this is fuelled by all sorts of humiliation built into an indiscriminate culture of rape. As in Genet's *Lady of the Flowers*, the dominant who penetrates the submissive is defined as uber-male, the submissive man as female. To be female is an extreme negative in this context, absolutely submissive in a manner that does not really ape heterosexuality except as parody. As a result, a brother gang member would feel deeply compromised when they take the submissive role but even the dominants are suspect. This is not a world of love. Violent antidotes are required purifications to the taint of violent homosexuality.

Of course most of this has rarely been made explicit in the classic Western. However, acts intending to inspire humiliation are very common. This stands in for rape in the Western. Since sex is humiliating for the submissive gang member, for the aggressive gang member, and for women who come in contact with the cattlemen —for the purest cattlemen always make certain that while they may not rape prostitutes they do humiliate them— sex is not really something that binds them, it is not even a twisted form of love. It must be noted that some movies will occasionally show scenes of tenderness by cattlemen, or they will make offers to turn the bad woman into an 'honest woman' by coming back and settling down. But placed in a distant future as they are, in the context of the movie, women are doomed to another fate: seduced and abandoned. The only expression of love allowed the cattleman (and any gang member) is in the form of loyalty. It is an enforced loyalty. Just as in *The Sopranos*, once you become part of the 'family' you can only leave by dying. Your loyalty is life-long and breaching it means death.

One can see other aspects of this by looking at other types of gangs. Rape features strongly in sports for example.

There have been several cases of well-known hockey players who have come forward in the last few years with stories of the abuse they suffered on junior teams. There is a connection between this man-boy rape and heterosexual rape that I think has to do with disgust. On one hand the rapists are disgusted with themselves, especially if they have been abused, and they are disgusted with girls and women, I think because boys, in high level hockey teams, spend too much time with other boys and not enough with girls. Elite teams foster a real delayed sexuality and a retarded maturity.

Even when we are little we have a notion of sex and it seems sort of ugly or disgusting. I think this continues into our teen years when our drive builds. Even pictures of nude men and women, especially the genitalia, seem ugly and instinctually dirty, I mean we piss and shit there. Some rape is propelled in part by revulsion. Immaturity and lack of contact with girls makes this worse. Boys are always joking about their own parts too and it demonstrates both a kind of homoeroticism and disgust. I am sure that boys who are molested are not always 'forced' in the sense of being pinned down and forcibly sodomized (though I am sure that happens all too often). More often than not it's a kind of disgusting ritual they must go through to get where they want to go.

When they were hazed they may have gone through other humiliating rituals in order to fit in with the team. Most of these rituals have to do with disgust. In fact, on the StopHazing.org website it lists as some examples of hazing: simulate sex acts; forced or coerced shaving of heads or other body parts; perform sex acts; public nudity; being paddled. It is well known there is perverse quid pro quo going on here. Rookies are threats but it is also payback time. While humiliation is the first object of hazing, the side effects of humiliation may involve associations of sex with it, or a discovery of a nascent sexuality, i.e. homosexuality, or perhaps worse, an association of sex with rape.

Men who live together without women, sailors, soldiers, or cattlemen are intimate with each other like one might be in a family or even more. Farting becomes a kind of game and they often piss together. And humiliation is *de rigueur* because ranking must happen. In many movies about men in gangs you will see a newby humiliated by middle ranking gang members then saved by the boss or a lieutenant, taken under his wing so to speak. If someone really crosses a line then he might get raped and this establishes a triumph and puts that guy in his place.

So when women come into the scene, these guys don't know what to do and, as well as putting on the bravado show of noticing ass, legs and tits, are vaguely disgusted by the prospect. So it takes on something of a prostitution or rape scenario. Prostitutes teach them sex but not the ways to be with an ordinary woman. And despite the bravado, going to a prostitute is deeply humiliating. You have to pay for sex! What's wrong with you? So prostitutes who want return business mother the johns and console them and tell them they are okay. In the context of a gang or a team, post-coitus with a prostitute, the man struts as though something was accomplished that enhances their masculinity when really they have been emasculated.

Scenes you get in movies involving such men often take on the characteristics of rape, if not all out rape. And this plays into a female fantasy as well; the bodice ripper. Women do desire this sense that a man is overwhelmed with lust for them, it speaks to their attractiveness. On the other hand they do not want to be raped in any real sense. While the distinction should be very clear, sometimes it can be muddled, and gang members lack the maturity and subtlety to navigate this territory.

There is a female corollary to the hockey team member and the gang member. They are the trophy wife and the bad girl. The former sees what can be gained by winning the oaf and the latter likes to play rough and just really likes the company of this kind of man, and perhaps feels protected by them.

Men in gangs suffer from the absence of tenderness. In 1974, Sean O'Callaghan while in Omagh, County Tyrone, "fatally shot Detective Inspector Peter Flanagan of the Royal Ulster Constabulary's Special Branch. D.I. Flanagan, a Catholic, was regarded as a traitor by both the IRA and many local residents. D.I. Flanagan was also rumoured, falsely, to have used excessive force while interrogating IRA suspects"[5] Son of an IRA man, O'Callaghan joined the Provos in 1970 at the age of 15, but by 1988 he had turned himself in to the police. He pleaded guilty to 42 crimes. He became an informer and turned down witness protection choosing to "take responsibility and make peace." He would be a man hated by both Unionist and Republicans.

His story and his books speak of a dehumanizing hatred that makes the enemy subhuman. Once in the gang there is no peace, no time for tenderness or love, just seething anger. It is, as it was for O'Callaghan, a life of hopeless terror with no reprieve. For him to have associated with anyone, in friendship or love outside the gang, would have made them a target. Relationships in a gang become only about the same kind of quasi-rape that we saw among the cattlemen in the Western and the gangster in the film noir. Love and tenderness always puts some at risk in the best of times, but in these situations it becomes about life and death.

In *Romeo and Juliet*, the archetypal romantic tragedy of gangs, we see precisely this. Love and tenderness between gangs puts everyone at risk of endless reprisal and unending murder and violence.

---

5. http://en.wikipedia.org/wiki/Sean_O'Callaghan. See also his book *The Informer* (Toronto: Bantam Press, 1998) for his whole story.

Integrity and Responsibility

L oyalty versus integrity. For me this forms one of the basic tenets of existentialism, i.e. integrity trumps loyalty. What does this mean? Simply put one upholds one's own personal values higher than one's loyalties. If a friend or family member does wrong you tell them so. In a case where a friend complains that so and so has wronged them and from what they tell you, you can see that they are the ones in the wrong, you say so. A close friend and an acquaintance are having a dispute but you know your friend is in the wrong, you say so. You speak up.

For those who believe in loyalty the opposite is true. A friend is always right in your eyes. A friend that does not stick up for you in cases like this is not a friend. The only support one can give friends is to continually give affirmation to their delusions about themselves. True loyalty would have a friend conspire with his/her friend even in their own downfall. But this is the most basic description of what I mean. To start, we need to flesh out the differences between loyalty and integrity and see how they intermingle.

There are obviously cases in real life where upholding loyalty or integrity with friends or family would be trivial and sticking to one principle over the other would be precious. This dynamic is played out with both farce and deadly seriousness in adolescence. A typical hypocrisy of which I was truly guilty as an adolescent was to pride myself on my own integrity while demanding the utmost loyalty of my friends. I suppose this might be the case with many of us. But one cannot have integrity and be a hypocrite, and since we are all hypocrites, none of us can claim integrity. The question becomes the manner in which we fail to retain integrity.

Pure loyalty would erase one's personality. One can sometimes see something akin to this in destructive relationships where one spouse's demand for loyalty destroys the other's personality. Absolute integrity would involve extreme loneliness and likely self-loathing. Living only through demands of loyalty placed upon one by friends and family would be a debilitating slavery to the approval of another. Integrity seems to require a sense of self-worth, but paradoxically it is also the reason for that sense of self-worth.

But to be loved unconditionally also fosters a feeling of self-worth. One is loved unconditionally by one's mother, by both parents when one is a baby. If one is not so loved then one suffers, and is wounded, perhaps permanently. At some point that unconditional love of a parent, from which one probably initially reflects back unconditional love, can sap from that same parent their autonomy as an individual, when the child nurtured to be independent moves away from solely that kind of approval. To be your own person, you need to make your own decisions and in doing so you move away from the unconditional love of one's parent. The parent, no longer embraced by unconditional love starts to ask for, or demand, loyalty from their children.

And this game is played out again by children with their friends and their teenage romances and so on. In each scenario they are divided against themselves by the loyalty that love demands and by the integrity that self-respect, self-love, demands.

There is no balance here; integrity must trump loyalty in the adult world. To love as an adult one must have self-respect. The only way to have self-respect is to respect a personal ethic and that ethic must be autonomous from loyalties of any kind. The definition of an adult friend is someone who respects the other's personal autonomy. Autonomy means the ability to live alone. This doesn't mean one can't live with other people, but that one's self-respect is not dependent on the approval of another. Seeking that approval is fine as long as it does not determine that ethic.

In order to be loved with integrity, one must have that self-love we call self-respect. The only way to have self-respect is to be able, when the time comes, to act according to one's ethic. To have self-respect also means that one does not require the loyalty of friends, otherwise it would not be self-respect, i.e. I only respect myself as much as others respect me or love me or are loyal to me. Rather, I respect myself whether friends are loyal or not, love me or don't. In doing so one makes oneself worthy of their respect.

The integrity/loyalty dynamic parallels that of the master/slave dialectic. To transcend the latter one must become a master without slaves. Similarly, to achieve integrity one must view all loyalties as conditional; one must be first and foremost loyal to integrity.

Shane strives for integrity, while the cattlemen and homesteaders are bound together in conflicting loyalties. Shane develops loyalties to the boy and his family, by stepping up and taking responsibility for their well-being. Shane also has some respect for the kind of freedom that the cattlemen remember and still want. And he knows the precarious doomed status of the gunslinger. What he realizes is that, if he stays, the family he has learned to care for will be divided by him and that the homesteaders will expect and demand he protect them, and that the cattlemen will not quit. Wounded, he leaves, hoping to regain his integrity. Existentialism is about, amongst other things, integrity. Existential integrity involves no bad faith, not being divided against one's self. This is expressed in corollary concepts of authenticity and responsibility. This is demonstrated in taking complete ownership of the totality of one's being, one's actions and their consequences.

The gang is primarily about loyalty. The tribe is primarily about loyalty. The homesteaders are about loyalty in the form of solidarity against threat. Shane is about integrity. Shane fails because integrity is impossible. Shane is an existential hero. The existential hero is doomed to failure. Shane seeks integrity because of a failure to be loyal. He is an outlaw, a man of the gun. He understands the cattlemen and their code of conduct, and he understands that disputes with gangs can only be settled with violence, and because of that form of dispute resolution there is no resolution. It is, in fact, violence without end.

As a very young boy I realized quite quickly that violence would only lead to more violence. That solving issues with punches would make an enemy sworn to revenge. As well, if one was to pick a fight with a gang member, and that included families, and win, one would from then on have to be on one's guard as vengeance could come at any time and from any member. I saw this in action with my father and his brothers; to wrong one was to wrong all.

In the scenarios I considered as a young boy, using equations necessary to calculate risk, humiliation was preferable to heroism. In the gang this is considered cowardice and cowardice would ultimately be the taunt used to humiliate. Another option might be to allow oneself to be beaten up but this was no escape from humiliation. Between the humiliation of defeat and that of cowardice, the latter has fewer repercussions. This either/or was as usual a no win situation. One can walk away to taunts of cowardice, or fight and win and fall prey to endless pursuit by older brothers, or join a gang and become their patsy, particularly by fighting. Either way offered little profit. These minor humiliations would pass, but violence offered an endless exchange.

In many stories, in movies, the 'standing up' to violence is seen as heroic. And in the more standard fare Western the good guy always wins, as though goodness was an unstoppable power. Superman's all-powerful goodness makes him dramatically uninteresting, so like Achilles there needs to have a 'weakness.' Kryptonite and threats to Superman's weaker friends and loved ones provide some drama, since his infinite ability provides little ethical interest or dramatic power. And so go many Westerns and similar genres where the inherent 'goodness' of the hero makes for a dull display. It is Shane's flaws, his absolute failure, that makes him interesting.

The only real play of philosophical interest in movies is when we have a character, a flawed one, striving for integrity, as in the case of classic noir movies like *The Maltese Falcon*. The only way that an incomplete integrity manifests the key moral questions is when it is compromised. The hero often comes out more broken than when he or she began. Perhaps we can only work towards integrity when we lose face.

Shane is an image of integrity because he is imperfect, tainted, failing and doomed. Those who think integrity is a kind of placid confidence misunderstand the consequences of their actions. Only by failing to take account for one's actions can one maintain a smug indifference that is definitely not integrity. Shane's own allegiance to integrity brings him to acts that in the end go against his beliefs, undermine his self-worth and ironically compromise him with loyalties. Humans seeking integrity must co-exist with hypocrisy. Loner or not, Shane's personal dignity has much to do with interaction with other people. The desire to act in a truly principled way condemns one to failure. The consequences of one's actions cannot be predicted.

Socially enforced morality works by suggesting that certain acts are always right and others are always wrong. This kind of moral agent is judged solely by how the acts are described. Do you tell the truth? Are you faithful to loved ones and family? You do not steal and so on. Acts are permitted or disallowed and require acts of contrition or punishment for lapses. These are loyalties, loyalty to family, religion, community, and nation. The Ten Commandments speak almost exclusively of loyalties, except for the prohibition against murder, though even murder may be required by integrity. This in essence is the modality of Greek tragedy.

For Shane, the consequences are what matter. He also realizes that most situations that require integrity will require more than the applicable moral tenet. The right action will undoubtedly entail very bad consequences. Doing the right thing, more often than not, will make one a pariah. Situations do not provide one with win-win possibilities, but inevitably with lose-lose. He also knows that integrity is not rewarded with peace of mind. That is because intentions do not excuse and consequences are unforeseeable. One can learn from one's mistakes, but avoiding previous mistakes only generates new mistakes.

Loyalties to families or gangs can make things seem correct. Most Westerns (indeed, most movies) are constructed as stories that suggest that the right action results in general goodness. The cowboy who comes home, settles down and starts a family suggests that all is right with the world; that moving from one kind of outdated loyalty, the cowboy life, to the new one, the one with a future, the family life of love and the law, is the happy end.

While Shane knows this will not work for him, he also knows that when he must leave at the end of the movie that it will not work for those he left behind. The little boy crying after Shane at the end is still under threat. The law, love and the family will not solve the problem. Violence only begets more violence. The gang may transform itself and become part of the community as when the Mafia becomes legitimate. In some Native tribes, they incorporate the band of brothers, ritualistically into the kinship structure, and this is what eventually happens to mavericks in more typical Westerns. But Shane, well, he cannot find a place here and still be Shane.

This is where Shane differs from the cattlemen, the gang, the band of brothers. The theme of the more classic Western, the ones that end like the *Odyssey*, with free-rangers and outlaws finding their way home to the arms of a good woman — is exactly where *Shane* differs. The free-ranging cowboy, the Marshall who was an outlaw, and other roamers and free spirits in Westerns, make the transition to domesticity. They can settle down. Even the most violent of cattlemen, as we have seen, have a place in their hearts for mother and a 'good' woman.

Cattlemen will often talk of getting their own 'spread.' A cattleman, cowboy, can imagine being fenced in at some later point. The free-rangers and the cattleman both operate on the modality of loyalty. The loyalty just has different content. The fierce loyalty of the gang enforced by violence can be translated into a loyalty enforced by law. The relations between a band of brothers can easily become familial. Loyalties to brothers can be adapted to loyalties to wives and children.

In many Westerns there is the implication that once the final fight has been won, that the hero can put down his gun. He can restrain his violence into support and protection for wife and kids. The brawler moves away from being someone where every conflict is worth deciding by violence to a father whose implied strength is just the power behind love, just as the law has power because it will use violence if necessary. The law and the family prefer to have rules and implied violence, to have codes and roles to solve conflicts. The son does rise up to overturn the father as might happen in a gang. One father does not challenge another and then take his wife and kids, as might happen between gang leaders.

The Fastest Gun Alive can be seen as the epilogue to *Shane*. In this movie, Glenn Ford tries to go where he's not known and live a normal life with his wife. He seeks domesticity and freedom from the responsibility of his past. He is, of course, found out and cornered. The town folk plead with him to protect them. And in doing so this whole dream of escaping the past and his responsibilities goes up in smoke. Called upon to act, the person of integrity is doomed to fail.

Shane also understands that the law and the love that the homesteaders would have him fall sway to, would demand a new loyalty. It would be a new loyalty in terms of the law that would expect him to set aside his own personal integrity to accept the arbitrary enforcement of abstract power. He would be acting on behalf of certain interests: property, state, church. He would be obliged to accept familial obligations and the happenstance of where love randomly finds its object. In love he would be acting first to protect the other and not what he thinks is right.

Shane intervenes on behalf of the weak. He sees the fight as unfair between the feminized homesteaders with their weak appeal to abstract law and the cattlemen who are unafraid to use outlaw violence to squash anyone in their way. He is standing on the fence in a situation that demands he choose sides. He refuses the opposition. He sees no natural moral superiority of either lifestyle. As a man of the gun he carries the burden of past bad acts, of having had to resort to violence. Whether he was a drifter, an ex-cattleman, or an ex-criminal, Shane seeks some kind of redemption. Yet he cannot accept the offer to settle down because he is both unworthy and because he would not be able to trade his dignity for the cosiness of family life. His sense of integrity requires the possibility of outlaw solutions. He won't stand passively by to threats of violence and thus cannot work within the law. He suspects the validity of the law. He cannot be a bystander. He must act. This not only means he lives under constant threat but that anyone connected with him will be as well. As a kind of avenging angel he cannot be compromised by the possibility of being held hostage to love.

Shane is not at peace with his power. He cannot abide the hypocrisy of either camp. He will not exchange his freedom for the sanction of the law. He is not naïve enough to believe in the purity of the law. It is a compromise, an exchange of the appearance of principle for order. He knows in whose interest the law operates. He is not willing to negotiate the ledger of good and evil the law purports to insure, that more good than bad will result. Shane realizes that the resolution he has brought is ephemeral. He is ashamed of having to resort to violence to quash the cattlemen, to have legitimized its use, because violence is the currency of the gang.

Shane represents integrity and integrity is always incomplete. Nevertheless, as a principle, it places highly unattainable demands on a person, demands the person of integrity is willing to accept. In this acceptance of the high demands of integrity, Shane accepts failure. Shane accepts the impossibility of integrity. And yet this is integrity, this failure. Integrity allows for the fact that no one will ever meet its demands.

The impossibility of integrity and the comforts of loyalty are at the crux of the story. In order to be free one must be responsible for the consequences of one's actions. There is no 'thing' to stand in one's stead, no circumstance to excuse one's behaviour; for to do so would undermine one's freedom. Shane is in a state of dread, standing on the edge of Kierkegaard's cliff, face to face with death, realizing the horrible burden of freedom. At this point, overwhelmed by responsibility, Shane stands for integrity against loyalty. He walks away rather than be bound by the compromised comfort of defeating the gang, or accepting the rewards of the hero, which would bind him even more. Integrity would become a nostalgic dream. Loyalty requires courage sometimes but only in the service of the group. You stand up for your own kind, your family, your gang, your race, and your nationality. When patriots speak of integrity they mean only loyalty, they mean no personal freedom, no self-conscious awareness of the other. Here ethics only pertain to us, not to them.

Shane knows that the homesteaders are not only encroaching on the freedom of the cattlemen, but also the Indians and people like him. They would absorb him. He walks away, but the homesteaders will eventually catch up with him and either jail him (put him on a kind of reservation) or kill him. They are no good guys here, no innocents. If Shane could find the wild and the free of Rousseau's transitional human, in that space between the conscious animal and civilizations, then it would be a different story. But it's over before it begins. It's not quite tragic because unlike Oedipus, Shane is conscious of the inevitability of the story. For Shane, being at home is not a little house on the prairie, it is being at home in the world. Wandering is as close as he will get to that. Shane comes out of nowhere and he goes back to nowhere.

Once Shane understands that he cannot stay, we also realize that the Western is not about rugged individualism in the sense of the petty bourgeois made good. Neither the cattleman nor the homesteader nor the lawman is a rugged individualist. All of these figures live and breathe loyalty. Ultimately, the homesteader family life lived under state enforced law is the ultimate telos of the Western. Even the free-range cattleman, representing a disruptive gang element with criminal and violent tendencies that threatens the homesteader, will ultimately come to coexist with the homesteader under the rule of law. Only Shane is separate. But he must forever live on the fringe of this society; Shane must go, wander, keep a low profile and ultimately be killed. He is not the foundational model for American capitalism that is and has always been corporatist. Shane stands against this gang as much as any other.

> ...for Kant, the illegal still falls within the category of legality — they both belong to the same register, that of things conforming or failing to conform with duty. Ethics — to continue the analogy — escapes this register. Even though an ethical act will conform with duty, this by itself is not and cannot be what makes it ethical. So the ethical cannot be situated within the framework of the law and violations of the law. Again, in relation to legality, the ethical always presents a surplus or excess.[6]

Shane's responsibility makes him an outlaw. The criminal behaviour of Wilson or the cattlemen cannot justify Shane's actions but the law itself is preventing the ethical. The ethical cannot be limited by the law. So those who stand idly by as the law is used to suppress or harm, as in limitations to citizenship by race or sexuality, fail to meet the demand.

> That is why the subject can be guilty (i.e. free to have acted otherwise) even though her actions were thoroughly determined by causal laws.[7]

For Kant, we cannot excuse ourselves because we were carried to actions by circumstances beyond our control. Each action Shane takes and any and all the characters, their powerlessness, the foolhardiness of the ex-Confederate soldier that takes on Wilson, people driven from their homes and burnt out, they all inevitably lead to Shane's actions. The film noir always has characters pushed in directions they did not intend to go, but they are not innocent, they are guilty.

---

6. Alenka Zupancic, *Ethics of The Real: Kant, Lacan* (London: Verso, 2000) p. 12.
7. ibid., p. 29.

Paradoxically, it is at the moment when the subject is conscious of being carried along by the stream of natural necessity that she also becomes aware of her freedom.[8]

Any greater evil that propels actions does not excuse us. The oil companies may be the driving force of destruction but we are all complicit whether we use oil or not. We let it happen. The unholy nefarious disease that holds corporations in its spell, is not the sole responsibility of the management or the stock holders.

Limited by its cinematic structure, even the anti-hero like Shane, is compelled to stand in for a kind of resolution. The film itself is ethically flawed and abandons Shane's impossible ethical demand. Even in the apparently unresolved ending the audience is set free by its mere formal cinematic resolution. It does not inspire probing ethical questions but rather delivers something more akin to post-coital lassitude.

Shane incarnates Kant's deconstruction of ethics as impossible in the face of the all too human tendency to pathology. We cannot do good for the sake of good but only for the sake of ourselves or for others or the honour it will bring us. In humans, ethics is undermined by the human need for approval and reward. This is what Kant calls pathology and opposes it to duty. Kant's duty must be pure, there can be no doing good in order to avoid pain of censure or to gain approval. One must do good only for its own sake. It is impossible for humans. Ethics is only possible for angels because angels are only agents and have no compassion or capability for love. The mother who sacrifices herself for her child does it for love, an angel will smite you without blinking an eye. This angel who can avoid pathology and seemingly represent true ethical behaviour is a true sociopath, he can only practice non-pathological ethics because he has no feelings, no kindness and is incapable of affection. The real problem with ethics is a theological one. There can be no freedom from pathology when the world is created by a being incapable of empathy. God is like a little boy picking wings off a fly and watching it suffer. God is Baby Huey. An infant who will crush people with a single blow if they say he can't have his way. At some point Abraham and Job should have told God to "fuck off," tortured as they were by the latter's need to show his power. These fables represent humans as mere playthings of God.

Shane is an existential hero because he bears and accepts responsibility for his actions. He does this completely and without condition, accepting any and all consequences, foreseeable or unforeseeable. His sense of integrity demands that he accept responsibility regardless of intentions. *Intentions don't matter, only consequences.* One might reply that he escaped responsibility by leaving, given

8. ibid., p. 27.

the inevitability of further threats to the homesteaders. Yes, but by weighing the full range of consequences Shane would only repeat the foolish courageousness that is a mark of loyalists represented in the film by the ex-Confederate soldier so coolly dispatched by Jack Palance. And secondly, as I pointed out above, settling in with the homesteaders would enslave Shane to the role of policeman, an integrity destroying role that involves conflicting and corrupting loyalties to the community, the law and the state.

As we have seen above, the intractable dilemma of integrity does not provide one with sturdy ethical axioms by which one can live. We are damned to live. If you are going to give preference to integrity you are bound to lose friends and not influence people. But you cannot therefore, like the nihilist, just spurn responsibility to others. To have integrity you must be willing to risk loving, and you must accept responsibility for any pain you inflict even if integrity demanded it. When circumstances demand it, you must step forward, but not from loyalty, popularity or patriotism, and you must expect to fail in almost every significant case. You are damned to fail but you cannot escape responsibility for these failures.

That sense of responsibility is shaped by love, especially that unconditional love a parent has for a baby. That love that has shaped the ideal of personal integrity in you, cannot only be for yourself, also not only for your parents, siblings, friends and colleagues, but must be for everyone. Your own demand for self-integrity entails that you respect the integrity of everyone. This is what I call 'absolute responsibility.' Integrity demands that there is no escaping responsibility. Love must be something more than the pleasure of knowing someone cares for you, that they stand as a symbol of your lovability, a testament that you are not indeed fungible and worthless. Love must mean that devotion is more than to one dear person, but to all. Personal integrity means recognizing in oneself that self-respect must mean that every person demands of you the same responsibility. There can be no self-respect without respect of the other, the former is tied to the latter.

There is no self-respect, no dignity without the respect of the inherent dignity of the other. To demean the other, to ignore their pain, to treat them as worthless, merely one of many is precisely to accept your own worthlessness. To be loved can only come from loving the other, which is why the rich and famous have such a difficult time of it. There is always, on one hand, the knowledge that one is utterly undeserving of adulation or wealth, and on the other hand that in all likelihood any 'love' coming one's way is due not to one's integrity as a person but merely to the desire of the other to be associated with wealth, fame or power. One is, in this case, a commodity, so fungible, exchangeable. Hence the anxiety generated therein.

The rich person may not be able to experience the love nor the integrity required for self-respect. While it is easier for a camel to get through the eye of a needle than a rich man to get into heaven, this sort of anxiety is one of the inherent side effects of civilization. As a consequence, self-respect's demand for absolute responsibility is played out as a game, we will always fail at. The choice for those living in the modern world as it stands is cynicism or to aspire and fail in the goal of self-respect. It is in this regard that I read Camus' *Myth of Sisyphus*. Yes constant failure, but still choose life over suicide.

And further as in Beckett:

"Ever tried. Ever failed. No matter. Try Again. Fail again. Fail better."

Rousseau in the Wild West

There is today a frightful disappearance of living species, be they plants or animals. And it's clear that the density of human beings has become so great, if I can say so, that they have begun to poison themselves. And the world in which I am finishing my existence is no longer a world that I like.

—Claude Lévi-Strauss[9]

The coming of the law, civil society and bureaucracy, and eventually the railroads, spelt an end to free-ranging cattlemen as much as to Native American societies. The cattlemen's fate, even as usurpers and aggressors, was the same as that of the plains Indians, virtual extinction. Plains Natives survive as a racial minority but their culture no longer has a context. Cowboys are now a kind of fashion statement and only survive in the tawdry spectacle of the rodeo. But the idea of the cowboy, especially as a free-ranging cattleman, is an archetypal figure for America. Indeed, the idea extends from Canada to Argentina, through almost all the Americas.

But behind the idea is a European one. It is an anti-enlightenment image that comes from Rousseau and was taken up by the Romantics. In the *Discourse on the Origin and Basis of Inequality Among Men*, Rousseau argues against civilization. He describes, in a thought experiment, the figure of a humanoid that lived between animal and what we now know as human. This is a figure that lives without anxiety and who is essentially self-sufficient; that lives and dies by his or her own wits. This figure, is a transitional figure, called the 'natural man,' but often confused with so-called primitive man[10]. Rousseau makes it clear that this figure of the natural man, no longer exists. He speaks of Native Americans as people who are closest to the natural man but already changed so much that he or she is much closer to us.

The natural 'savage,' as Rousseau called him, lives at a moment in evolution after pure animal but before human culture. There is no questioning of purpose. While life could be difficult it was not because the savages had to convince anyone of their worth. Their survival was there around them, ready at hand. They only needed to satisfy basic needs. This might be difficult but they had the tools, their own bodies, to survive. Once their needs were satisfied, they were free to do what they pleased. There is no asking why there is something rather than nothing, no need of philosophy or religion or self-justification. (Because Rousseau remarked

9. http://www.npr.org/templates/story/story.php?storyId=120066035
10. I am using 'man' in this context because I am drawing mainly on Rousseau's text. His main point is that there was once a human who was self-sufficient. He uses 'man' in this sense where human would perhaps be more appropriate. Anything said here would apply to females of the same era. See below where I discuss the anthropology which emphasizes virtually no sexual division of roles.

about the Native American being closer to a state of nature than the European, many have wrongly conflated the true savage with the Native American. When Rousseau speaks about the transition from savage to cultured man, and defines them, one can see that any description of the Native as Rousseau's savage person is wrong.)

The Wild West became a show almost immediately after its death. As early as 1836 painter George Catlin charged an entrance fee to see his paintings of the Wild West. Very soon after that he brought live Indians with him to perform music and dance, horse tricks, faux scalping, erect wigwams for Eastern audiences and eventually took the show on to Europe. Later, Catlin reconsidered and fought to ban such shows which became ever more popular. Eventually Buffalo Bill Cody extended the popularity in an even coarser form. And there is a direct connection from the Wild West show to the movie business.[11]

The Wild West show portrayed a world that had already disappeared. By Rousseau's time Amerindians had been brought to Europe to meet royalty. The slave trade was in full swing and Africans had also arrived in Europe at the same time. Rousseau was not interested in the spectacle of the primitive. The current savages were noble by comparison with Europeans because most were still imbued with a kind of dignity that comes from self-sufficiency, from knowing how to survive by their own hands. He also recognized that they had suffered greatly from contact with Europeans.

Now, I really would like someone to explain to me what type of misery there could be for a free being whose heart is at peace and whose body is healthy. I ask the following: Which is more subject to becoming insupportable for those who enjoy it, a civil or natural life? Around us we see hardly any people who do not complain about their existence and several who even take their own lives to the extent they are capable of that, and the combination of divine and human laws is scarcely sufficient to check this disorder. I ask if anyone has ever heard it said that a savage at liberty has so much as dreamed of complaining about life and of killing himself. So people should judge with less pride on which side true misery lies.[12]

With a simple and solitary life, very limited needs, and the implements which they had invented to provide for those needs, men enjoyed a

11. I am indebted to Peter Wollen's essay "The Myth of The West" from *Paris Manhattan: Writings on Art* (London: Verso, 2004) pp. 182-201.

12. http://records.viu.ca/~johnstoi/rousseau/seconddiscourse.htm, or Jean-Jacques Rousseau, *The Basic Political Writings* (Indianapolis: Hackett, 1987) p. 52.

great deal of leisure and used it to gather several types of commodities unknown to their fathers. And that was the first yoke they unwittingly imposed on themselves and the first source of the evils they were preparing for their descendants. For, apart from the fact that in this manner they continued to weaken their bodies and minds, since these commodities, through habit, lost almost all their charm and, at the same time, degenerated into real needs, the lack of them became much crueler than the sweetness of possessing them, and people were unhappy to lose them without being happy to own them.[13]

Without my prolonging these details to no purpose, everyone should see that, since the bonds of servitude are not formed except by the mutual dependency of men and by the reciprocal needs which unite them, it is impossible to enslave a man without previously putting him in a situation where he is unable to do without someone else. Since this condition does not exist in the state of nature, it leaves each man in it free of the yoke and makes the law of the strongest ineffective.[14]

This 'time' that Rousseau, has imagined, of the nobility of natural humans, is for me what I call, not without some cheek: 'The Wild and the Free.' There is a scene in the movie *The Edukators*[15], where Jule talks about living "wild and free." That moment in that film captures what Rousseau is getting at. Whether there is stage in human evolution that is precisely like that is not all that important, the notion is so universal and so resonant that it does not matter. I think though, there is something in all of us that pines for the wild and the free and when we dream of this we know how false and bankrupt our current social relations are.

13. http://records.viu.ca/~johnstoi/rousseau/seconddiscourse.htm, or ibid., p. 63. Here Rousseau has already seemed to see the creation of a proto-buyer's regret, see below for more on buyer's regret.
14. http://records.viu.ca/~johnstoi/rousseau/seconddiscourse.htm, or ibid., p. 59.
15. Here is the setup for the film from Wikipedia: "Jule is a waitress struggling to pay off the €100,000 debt she accumulated after crashing into a Mercedes-Benz S-Class of a wealthy businessman named Hardenberg (Burghart Klaussner) on a motorway. After she is evicted for paying her rent too late, she moves in with Peter and Jan, who are often out all night. When Peter takes a trip to Barcelona, Jan reveals that he and Peter spend their nights "educating" upper-class people by breaking into their houses, moving furniture around, and leaving notes with messages that say "die fetten Jahre sind vorbei" (the days of plenty are over), or "Sie haben zu viel Geld" (you have too much money). After learning about this, Jule convinces the reluctant Jan to spontaneously break into Hardenberg's home in the affluent Berlin suburb of Zehlendorf, as he happens to be away on business. During the break-in, the thrill of the moment entices the two to kiss. Jan leaves Jule alone for a few minutes because he does not want to hurt his friendship with Peter." During this second scene Jule asserts her desire for the "wild and free." From this notion I take my title for this book as the two concepts, wild and free, are co-dependent but from our civilized point of view (and Rousseau's) the further we are from the wild the less free we are. This obviously is a concept incompatible with capitalism, modernism, religion, consumerism, and Marxism, though Marx does vaguely hint at this as the end goal.

There is a sense in which the Western represents a dream world where the wild and free is almost available. It is always disappearing in these movies, receding into horizon. The cattlemen certainly represent aspects of it, the freedom of wandering and adventure. The Native Americans represent aspects of it, certainly the idea of sustainability and that people can survive without wage labour, rather cynically presented like a commercial for a resort in *Dances With Wolves*. Shane represents the lone individual as yearning for freedom. He is particularly appealing in his ability to walk away. Each of these archetypes in the Western present not the real image of that wild and free, but a kind of yearning for it and a simulation of it allowed in a time and place outside the law. It is also clear that the homesteaders do not represent, in any way, the wild and the free. They are civilization.

The cattlemen, Shane and the Indians are distortions of the idea of the wild and the free. Within the bounds of the Western they are images of relative wildness, relative to the homesteaders and Europeans. They appeal to that yearning in us. The actual outlaws, cattlemen and cowboys, and all sorts of other adventurers, pirates, wanderers, hobos, petty criminals, incarnate that evolutionary memory of the wild and the free, of being self-sufficient, perhaps ruthless but more completely alive. They are, of course, only incomplete imitations of what Rousseau is getting at. They invert the idea of the wild and the free when they bring into it aspects of the Hobbesian nightmare, the all against all. And because these manifestations usually degenerate into that family inversion, the gang, they invert, as well, the sought after wildness and freedom, into an us-against-them brutality, and a slavish devotion to groups and head dogs. While the impetus to this life was to move away from bondage of society, duty, politeness towards a spontaneous expression of the self, it is perverted in the gang into a group-think that can only be dissolved in the death of the gang or the member.

USA – Life, Liberty
and the Pursuit of Happiness

The USA was born of Enlightenment thought and many of its founding fathers were deeply influenced by French philosophy. Though Rousseau was not truly an enlightenment thinker (he is the first anti-enlightenment thinker), it seems clear that he influenced Jefferson. The influence was that of the Rousseau who had resigned himself to the realities of politics, Rousseau-qua-political philosopher. It bypasses Rousseau's deep suspicions about the possibility of freedom within the civilized world. Rousseau in this guise, accepting some regretful realities, looks to make the best of a bad situation.

The USA of these golden mythic days of Jeffersonian democracy is already a compromise of the freedoms that America promised to so many disenfranchised émigrés described on the Statue of Liberty. All those utopian communities, Fabian socialists, Quakers, Amish, Shakers, Levellers, all the crackpot religions and dreamers that saw America as the holy land were too late. These folks deeply informed the big myth of America, but also the frontier and the Wild West, from Shakers to Wobblies, from Cotton Mather to Mother Jones, the Branch Davidians, and the Unabomber.

The reality of European theocracy meant that atheists and freethinkers like Galileo, Spinoza and Rousseau had to hide under some religion, skulk about and publish in Holland or England, speak in tongues, tap dance around theology. For some, religious sects provided some shelter. They would insist that they, the non-believers fed up with the hypocrisy, were in fact a new kind of believer. You still put your life at great risk by trying this gambit in Europe, but America, well that was the land of hope for all the non-conformists, a term, of course, that originally had religious meaning. And so they came in droves to America, the place with ten thousand religions. Anybody could start their own religion in America, even now, we have new sects like:

- *The Followers of the Invisible Hand* — neo-con free market followers of Milton Friedman,
- *The Swingers* (update of Shakers) — polyamorous followers of Larry Flynt,
- *The Inhalers* — devotees of the Holy Hashish.

The inherent craziness of American culture, called a melting pot (though the fire is not hot enough to do much melting), has to do with the "self-evident truth" of the right to "Life, Liberty and the pursuit of Happiness." Jefferson's original formulation for the Declaration of Independence was, "We hold these truths to be sacred and undeniable . . . " He moved to a more secular construction from a religious one, i.e. "We hold these truths to be self-evident." This, in fact, made the rights broader in concept because they were based on human thought and did not depend on the sacred. If you consider Rousseau's original human, the one between the ape and civilization, you also have a conceptualization of freedom without any theological trappings. The right to life, liberty and the pursuit of happiness sound like discrete elements but they are interdependent. What is life without liberty and the pursuit of happiness? Life without those things is in fact the civilized hell that Rousseau took a stand against. It is not a right to happiness, only its pursuit. It is not a right to a happy life, but it is a right to life and liberty that includes the liberty to fail. Obviously one will fail to achieve happiness but one cannot be prevented from pursuing it.[16]

The "Pursuit of Happiness," as premise, sets the American myth on a path which draws more from Rousseau than the Enlightenment. It is not a goal that a government can provide a positive support for. It is principally an anti-government anarcho-bomb placed inside the constitution of a state. It therefore, somewhat ironically, emphasizes the real contingency of the state. It undermines theocracy at the get go. What is profoundly ironic is that the USA, as it currently exists, is for all intents and purposes a theocracy in action. The religion is a quasi Judeo-Christian patriotism. Like all theocracy it bases inequality and privilege on scripture.

So on one hand you have the American Dream, which says that all people can find happiness, and on the other, American Patriotism, which says that 'my country right or wrong' patriotism is built into the constitution. The way the pursuit of happiness has been interpreted by the Church of American Patriotism is that the cream rises to the top. In other words, those who have wealth and power, have it because they are blessed, because they deserve it. Those who do not have wealth and power do not deserve it. And even though we know they will mostly fail, they can give it a shot. The pursuit of happiness becomes just a dream, something we see in the movies, but get real buddy, you're just going to have to suck it up and realize you're stuck in a dead-end. It's the Old Testament vengeance that inspires a savage inverted meritocracy in the USA: you don't win wealth because you deserve it, you deserve it because you have it.

16. I could never abide Liberation Theology because theology is the basis for all authoritarianism. There is no liberation in Christ. That's why I find Terry Eagleton's mining the tidbits of socialism in Jesus and Paul rather pathetic. Feuerbach understood this. The thing is, liberation theology is Luther not Catholicism, i.e. the protest aspect of Protestantism. Protestantism is at the root of the Diggers and Levelers. And this is not biblical really, it's philosophical, i.e. you take certain tenets of the Bible and you ask questions like, "Why is the Pope rich when Jesus was a carpenter's son?" and "Why are there huge expensive churches filled with gold where the congregations are mostly poor?" There is a kernel in the Bible, but it's situational ethics not Christian first principles that starts this. Theology can only lead to theocracy, hence America the ideal: freedom of religion requires separation of church and state and implies freedom from religion. One cannot be bound to religion by birth *and* chose it. So one of the choices has to be atheism. The Declaration of Independence is the founding document of atheism: "We hold these truths to be self-evident."

Many of the founding fathers would have rather not seen such a promise installed in the constitution or such inflammatory language as "All men are created equal…" They accepted that such noble ideals were necessary to keep the masses enthralled. But that ideal — the pursuit of happiness — with its Rousseau-like romanticism, is like a festering sore that won't go away. Americans still demand that their government give them happiness. Most critical thinking people realize that it ain't forthcoming, as those who govern have wholly different agendas than passing laws to increase happiness for anyone except for the rich and powerful.

And yet the government cannot sidestep this. This idea that government should be concerned with the happiness of ordinary people, that it should foster this pursuit, is an idea that has taken permanent hold of the American imagination. It is now a demand that governments must manage. It is a demand which marketers take ownership of, and promote a world of happiness as being a world of things, gadgets, cars, clothes, games, booze. So the libertarian right deals with the pursuit of happiness by saying that the holy mother market will provide everything for all the good children, i.e. the ones with jobs and credit cards.

But still, that happiness bit ain't satisfied with commodities or even those new age quasi-spiritual enlightenment services. It wants the whole of it, life, liberty AND the pursuit of happiness. My life is my own autonomous sphere. My liberty is freedom from the distractions of market exchange; that I can live independent of property and be self-sufficient. This is liberty and happiness. In America the idea has become that this form of liberty and happiness can only be bought. To attain it one must be independently wealthy. There is a big lie here, one that flies in the face of many of those communities that made up a large part of America, the dissenters, those religious groups who were fleeing religious persecution. A feature of many of these religions was poverty, self-sufficiency and independence. They were groups who had already turned their back on the clerics of state religion in Europe and had suffered persecution at their hands, from the Catholic mainland and the English quasi-Catholicism where the King of England is the 'pope.' In America these dissenters hoped to find freedom from persecution.

Buyer's Regret

The expansion of consumerism has turned frustration into the soul of the market and a spectacle where acquisition and representation of goods make illusory compensation for the lack of life. Dissatisfaction with what is bought is in fact supplemented with dissatisfaction at what cannot be bought. Existence which is identified with having has at every time stirred up the torments of jealousy, the rancour of envy, the bitterness of covetousness, and so as poverty increases and prohibits thoughtless expenditures it becomes evanescent like a shade in the land of the dead. The frenzy of possession has so thoroughly dispossessed living beings and things themselves that frustration urges them furiously to consume themselves until the extinction of the world.

—Raoul Vaneigem, *A Declaration of the Rights of Human Beings.*[17]

In his *Discourse on Inequality*, Rousseau describes some of the early transition from savagery to civilization. He describes how tools created to reduce work became needs, proto-commodities. What Rousseau is describing here is 'buyer's regret.' Buyer's regret is essentially the modern condition of alienation.

The 'natural' man that Rousseau is discussing is the so-called missing link. It is the stage between ape and human. It represents a kind of deep memory of us as nascent humans. Of course Rousseau would have no knowledge of this sort of evolutionary theory, his concept is more of a thought experiment to try and deal philosophically with a deep hypocrisy in human life. What forms the basis for this thought experiment is his *Discourse on the Sciences and the Arts*. This essay was written for a contest to address the question: "Has the reestablishment of the sciences and the arts served to purify or corrupt morals?"[18] To which he answered that the Sciences and Arts were the former; corrupting. Rousseau's work is, in the midst of the Enlightenment, the first *Civilization and Its Discontents*. Here, in a period so properly connected to the rise of a humanist and scientific culture, Rousseau is already critiquing the supposed benefits in a manner which is more trenchant and well-considered then reams of vacuous verbiage of so-called post-modernism; the have your cake and eat it too school of moribund academic critique.

In the essay that followed, *The Discourse on Inequality* (which is, in my view, superior to *The Social Contract*), he lays out a subtle but even more devastating critique of civilization. This being, the natural man, the pre-civilized human, is capable of surviving on his or her own. They have no schedule. They can forage and feed themselves without the help of others. They serve no master and follow no agenda. They are free in a profound sense that we cannot even understand. Though Rousseau just imagined that there must be a transitional period in order

---

17. *A Declaration of the Rights of Human Beings,* (London: Pluto Press, 2003) p. 107.
18. Rousseau, op.cit., p. 1.

to come to understand how we became so unfree, it is easier to suppose now, with the idea of evolution, a period of awareness of such freedom in human pre-history. In other words, a stage in our evolutionary development.

It might be fanciful to imagine a memory of this, but are we not all somewhat befuddled by the fact that we cannot survive without others, without society, capitalism, etc.? Does it not seem prima facie true that we should, by all accounts, be able to survive on our own without need of others, without the need to prove our value to others, to enter into some kind of compromised exchange of our time for someone else's money? Animals require nothing but the environment they are born into. We seem to require endless support to survive. I am sure that most people every day question why they spend so many hours in someone else's service, following someone else's agenda. "Man is born free, and everywhere he is in chains." Indeed![19]

When we imagine the concept of freedom, what do we imagine? Do we not imagine a life without schedule, agendas, work, commuting, shopping, etc.? We imagine what we felt as children, where a summer day unfolded before us infinitely, with only endless possibility and freedom. Children's dreams of adventure are of adventure without patronage, to be a wanderer, a hobo, an explorer, someone who can survive on their own wits. Huck Finn.

What Rousseau imagined was something even more free than an adventurer like Odysseus, who only represented the freedom within a frame, his time far from home. Rousseau calls to mind a stage when we were all free to wander. He denies Hobbes' deduction that without government it would be all against all. It is possible to be killed by an aggressor or an animal, but it is not a life of constant warfare. We can run or we can fight. It is up to us.

This notion of freedom is a platform for our dreams and the source of our discontent. We cannot shake this idea that we should go as our heart sees fit. Why do we need a house? Why do we have to buy land or rent it? Why should we buy food? And why do we have work? This is especially poignant when we acknowledge that work is primarily for the benefit of someone other than ourselves. It takes away far more than it gives in return. And this lack of freedom is a source for a life filled with anxiety. Rousseau would also add that this lack of freedom is directly related to the entrenchment of inequality.

Buyer's remorse, also called buyer's regret, is a kind of anxiety caused by doubts about the wisdom of any purchase. There can be a feeling that one has been duped by a sales person or by promotion. It can also be associated with

---

19. Some current anthropology does indicate that in the transition to becoming human, a stronger dependency on families and small social groups were necessary for certain changes to occur. Rousseau's conception is an entirely solitary being. The critical point is that, in general, pre-agricultural humans had the ability to fend for themselves, i.e. to survive by themselves. This gives a real sense of power and independence —which is dignity.

crowd behaviour; a person feels lacking because 'everyone' has a blender except them. The converse is also true; regret can be caused by the sense that one has not been independent and merely 'followed the crowd.'

There can be a feeling of loss once the money has changed hands. As a kid, a relative gives you $5 and you imagine a myriad of choices, endless possibilities. Once you settle on a purchase you no longer have any money and the world is limited to your solitary choice. On the other hand, too many choices creates remorse because one can now imagine that one has missed out on a better choice. This is called the 'paradox of choice.' More choices create more opportunities for regret. One can either worry that the one not chosen was indeed better or be persuaded of the same by a friend who has chosen the alternative. A further paradox to this is that the friend's assertion, that their choice was indeed a preferred one, can be driven by their own buyer's remorse, i.e. they have doubts and hope to feel better by convincing you that their choice was superior.

This can spiral out of control. People buy multiple versions of the same product to cover all bases, arguing that each is good for some situation, or that some convenience is gained. Or they buy and return, essentially testing each choice. Sometimes people may feel that their anxiety might be quelled by reading reviews or assessments of products or by using reference materials like *Consumer Reports* or *Lemon Aid*. Here there is either an appeal to authority or validation through popular vote. For instance, Elvis Presley's album, *50,000,000 Fans Can't Be Wrong,* would seem to be a safe bet. The internet has made this kind of information instantly available and free for the most part. But one can look at the massive amount of activity on the internet and see, not solace, but intensification of the anxiety and regret caused by consumerism. For every calm discussion about certain purchases, sometimes aided by experts who may have nothing but good intentions, there is a staggering amount of nasty posturing and abuse. In fact, most forums on the internet are an endless documentation of buyer's regret.

There is an argument to be made that some of this is a release valve for buyer's regret, whether it takes the form of venting on how crappy the item purchased is or what an idiot you are for having purchased that crappy piece of shit. And sometimes people come together to alleviate their sorrow by commiserating with other people who feel conned. Whether one takes the stance of always affirming one's purchases no matter what or of complaining about them, both are, in effect, manifestations of buyer's remorse.

Not just the paradox of choice but enforced and/or planned obsolescence just further exacerbates buyer's regret to the point that the more we buy the more we want. Just as, with regard to food, our eyes are bigger than our stomachs, we cannot find satisfaction in our purchases. One may have felt proud, in 1968, for the purchase of a colour television, and the feeling would have lasted because it would be a decade or more before the TV was replaced. But now it is as though the moment one arrives home with one's 72 inch LCD, we hear that the thinner

LEDs are here. And they are better in so many ways, so it's hard to feel good about the LCD, especially how thick it is. This is because, of course, with electronics, some element of miniaturization is important for satisfaction, even though not so long ago enormous CRTs or rear projection TVs requiring delivery vans and strong men, removals of doors and windows, were indications of status.

And writing this, one feels overwhelmed with cliché. To spell this out in such a way is only to indicate how old one is, and perhaps how irrelevant one is. Planned obsolescence is the cornerstone of 20th Century business and marketing, and in the 21st Century it only seems to have intensified. Even given buyer's remorse and its attendant psycho-social ills, this state of affairs seems 'natural.' The evanescent pleasure of buying is dwarfed by the regret and ennui that follows it. Buyer's remorse has become our state of being because buying is our primary activity. Buying things is our second job. We all know that shopping is hard work. While marketers want to portray that their products are conveniently delivered to us, it is us that are conveniently delivered to them.

As an example of 'buying is hard work,' look at the random consumer faced with 20 stores in the local mall selling sweaters. They are all essentially the same, maybe made in the same factory in Bangladesh, but we work hard to find the very subtle differences only to find ourselves faced with difficult choices. One store has 2 for $30, but because of the limited selection there the only choices would be blue and yellow, while the other store has blue and purple ones for $40. I like the blue one in the first store and the purple one in the other. If I buy single sweaters it will cost me $50 and I will get the ones I like but I will spend more. If I don't, I'll have a sweater I don't really care for. What to do? Ah, might as well buy all four. When I go home I see before me 38 sweaters, 20 of which I never wear because I don't like them after having bought them in previous sales. And then there is the credit card bill…

Credit is a new form of taxation which reverses the social welfare state into a living debtor's prison. Any reduction in taxes is a direct transfer of wealth from the poor to the rich. The rich float the speculative market because they suffer a critical mass of buyer's regret, since everything sold to them is a giant scam, from gourmet food (the waiters still spit in it) to art (the artists still shit in it), so they vent their frustration, at the vacuity of wealth, on the poor by burdening them with debt. You lose social services but here's $250,000 worth of credit. So they consume pizza and beer for every meal, become obese and have surgery that makes them millionaires of debt. Medical companies sell them their anti-depressants, bone replacements, diabetes monitors and fake breasts. All done up to the nines, there's massive depression brought on by a monstrous form of buyer's regret. In a way, from food to medical devices, there is a dismantling of responsibility and personal autonomy. Everyone says, 'do not tell me what to do,' while we all buy the exact same shit. Someone says that carrying around a computer device with music on it is an easily financed form of happiness, but this is really a kind of technological loneliness. Facebook is a loneliness machine. It is massively popular because it purports to solve isolation but it reeks of desperation.

Being so apparently totally connected to a billion people as we are, brings no satisfaction because we are all a kind of speck of dust. Our best relationships are with a few people, but knowing there's six billion people out there and being immersed in cultural mass of immense proportions can only isolate us, being one of 28,567 people who like Terry Eagleton is not satisfying. What is the purpose of culture? If there are 200 people being punks in Brixton they might even feel something like a community, but if there are 2 million people around the globe doing it, the connection becomes stylistic; form over content. Our happiness is probably tied to something we had 100,000 years ago, a strong connection of mutuality with 30 or 40 people. Our unhappiness increases proportionally to the extent of our technologically simulated interconnectedness.

Another great source of our buyer's regret is the size of the pile of garbage we create. This is a kind of soul crushing burden that many people are in denial about. They talk about it, and you know it bothers them, but it's really hard to take responsibility for it. If we attempted to do so it would be like widespread catatonia or hysteria. Perhaps, in a sense, this what we have. Our daily lives have become cycles of catatonia and hysteria. In vain attempts to deal with the guilt of garbage, we de-clutter. This means we take possibly perfectly good items, things we bear a fetishistic attachment to (the loss of which will make us more depressed), and throw them out, creating more garbage, but now we have more space to fill with more shit we don't need.

Another way to look at buyer's regret is to examine Levinas' concept of 'longing' as described by Drew M. Dalton in his book: *Longing for the Other: Levinas and Metaphysical Desire.*[20] Dalton states that, according to Levinas, we have this undefined longing for something that we cannot identify. We are not satisfied. We have a metaphysical desire that we attempt to fill. We can attempt to fill it with religion, or consumerism. Is it a lack or a perceived lack? Is this longing not related to anxiety? Is anxiety the sense of missing, losing or immanent doom? Is it based on disappointment? Perhaps also the anticipation of disappointment? Anticipation is like a deceptively good form of anxiety: I can't wait! Anxiety is the result of the continual disappointment of the anticipation, and this just increases the yearning.

In self-sufficiency our primary experience is plenitude, coming from understanding our environment and confidence in our ability. One might be tempted, in this sort of existential mode of thinking, to establish a permanent metaphysical lack as constituent of humanity, that longing and anxiety are rather profound modes of experiencing our own finitude. Though we might want to limit the mode of living we call consumerism to modernity, it is really just the

---

20. Drew W. Dalton, *Longing for the Other: Levinas and Metaphysical* Desire (Pittsburgh: Duquesne University Press, 2009).

mode of deferment in life we call agriculture, from which follows the feelings of inadequacy and the desperate mode of thinking we call hope or religion. In this mode, self-sufficiency is supplanted by a constant need, and periods of gluttony.[21] When the item does not fulfill by its mere possession, we infer that more of the same will fulfill. Quantity becomes quality.

A quality desired is substituted by a placeholder for that quality, and then the quality becomes divided again and again since we believe that if one car is good then 2 cars are better. And so whatever quality (say its usefulness) the car is meant to provide is meant to be multiplied, i.e. 2 useful modes of transportation is better than just one, in fact, there is still only one 'good' provided by the car. So in fact, 2 cars doesn't really double the usefulness, it divides the real value: ownership. Each car's value is divided psychologically to less than half. This is because once the first car was bought it has already lost the pure plenitude of the desired object. It was already less than what we wanted when we got it and 2 does not make twice as much joy but divides each in half, or less than half because both have already lost their glamour in the act of purchase. In the act of purchase we change the NEW (note that we usually say 'brand new' where branding is part of the 'value') into the USED. The used is tainted because someone already sucked most of the pleasure out of by buying it.

---

21. Lent follows Christmas.

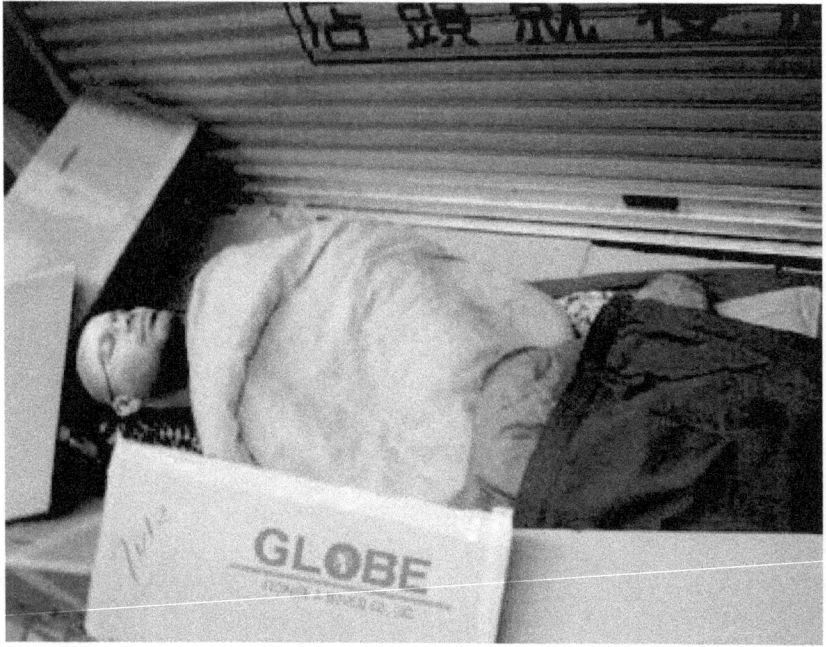

Homelessness

Bodies sleeping on the ground could evoke something good and natural; why
now do they connote the immanence of tragedy.

—David Hecht & Maliqalim Simone,
Invisible Governance: The Art of African Micropolitics[22]

So much of our lives are purchased. There are constant transactions. One is
work, where we trade our time for a wage. Another is called home, but it is
the negation of that. Why is it we must pay to have a home, a place of our
own? We take such fantastically inane ideas completely for granted. 'It's just the
way it is.' Contrast this with the natural human who is at home in the world.
What a bizarre idea that we have homeless people. They are homeless because
there is nowhere for them to go that some form of ownership has not proscribed,
so everywhere they go they trespass and some troll demands his toll. Is it harder
to imagine a time when such nonsense did not exist than it is to realize we live in
a world where there is no home, that because someone cannot find a job moving
paper or packing widgets, they become a kind of litter on our streets, a problem
we need to clean up?

Asking such questions will immediately brand you as unrealistic, a dreamer,
a communist, a hippie, a freak, deluded, insane. Now that we have surveyed every
inch of the land on our planet and made sure that it belongs to someone, some
corporation, some government, we want to do the same with the oceans and the
air. If you think about this for a moment, is it not clear that the only way there
could be land as property is that someone stole it in the first place? Would not
even the most hard-nosed capitalist or macro-economist have to admit that there
was a time without land as property?

How does one come to terms with the fact that one is born into a world
where one is already beholden to the descendants of thieves? And that one cannot
just live in the world using one's wits to feed and shelter one's self rather than beg
for a job doing something that does not benefit oneself in exchange for tokens
that one will give to someone else for shelter that one could build oneself and for
food that one could grow or find or hunt. I think it is fair to say that there was a
time when humans experienced a very different kind of life that was not "nasty
and brutish," though it might certainly have been short. It is also true that this
idea, however perverted by dreams of wealth or RRSP independence, informs
our dreams and that is why Shane appeals.

In current times we have a fantastically insane idea of the homeless. And to
be homeless is no longer to be free to roam but to be criminally insane, useless and

22. David Hecht & Maliqalim Simone, *Invisible Governance: The Art of African Micropolitics* (Brooklyn: Autonomedia, 1994), p. 142

unproductive. What an amazingly strange idea is this, that you can be born into the world and be homeless, criminal and subhuman, or that you can become that way. To be homeless represents a sin of sloth to those whose productive lives are made up of people turning their time into someone else's profit. Or to be those happy few who profit from the former's indentured life of misery.

We know why this is so and we just accept it. We learn to scorn the shiftless ragamuffins panhandling for cheap booze with a smug satisfaction that we are making something of ourselves. By what measure do we judge the value of life in this bizarre view? We accept that we are incapable of living by our wits and that freedom is just something like winning the lottery or having a fortune in RRSPs.

Why do we not stop for a minute and ask ourselves about this idea of homelessness? What can this mean? It means we have inverted reality. To have a home means to pay some form of rent. It is only by mapping every square inch of the world into private and public ownership that we have this kind of insanity. Not even the park is a free place. If you don't pay rent you belong nowhere!

The Occupy movement, regardless of its glaring faults, represents a new contestation of public/private space. As with the so-called homeless and gypsies, we have a concept of free-range coming up against a world where no land is not owned or policed. This condition is a direct result in North America of the Indian Wars and the homesteader/free-range conflict, both of which are integrally intertwined. It is a continuation of the brutal suppression of peasant uprisings in Europe which in turn led to that idea of America that drew these same folks to its shores. A place where that memory of the wild and the free could be reclaimed, where nomadism was possible again (it was 'uninhabited'!).

In America there is this myth of space and of free land. And of course this often brings up John Locke's *Two Treatises on Government* as justification for British imperialism in America. Along with this is the concept of *vacuum domicilium*, essentially the idea of an empty place and we see this in the Western, for both cattlemen and homesteaders. Locke has put forward the idea that land possession is derived from a person doing something with land, or as he says it, mixing her labour in with the land, i.e. planting. As a result the planter would own the land. Some have used this idea to justify the British and Americans pushing Native peoples off land that from their perspective, they had not done anything with or that natives had not realized the inherit value of.

But old John Locke is getting rather battered here for something he did not really say. He did see property as coming into being for the Native as they mixed their labour with the land, and they therefore claim possession. Furthermore, Locke did not endorse the idea of *vacuum domicilium*. In fact, he makes the case for the opposite, as stated below Locke is saying Native people can never be disinherited by conquerors.

No damage therefore, that men in the state of nature (as all princes and governments are in reference to one another) suffer from one another, can give a conqueror power to dispossess the posterity of the vanquished, and turn them out of that inheritance, which ought to be the possession of them and their descendants to all generations....¶184

Their persons are free by a native right, and their properties, be they more or less, are their own and at their own disposal, and not at his. ¶194[23]

A toddler might ask this question: "Why do they have no home?" At a modern level of alienation this question might tug at our heart a bit, but we still just walk on by. Why not buy them a meal? Offer them a bed?

These questions imply only partial answers in the shape of charity, acts which increase the indignity in many ways. The real question is: "How can a person be born into the world and be homeless?" We don't say the same of an elephant or a shark, even though in a different way they are becoming homeless as we speak. No product of evolution, no sentient being can realistically be homeless except in the perversion of modern civilization. One could play the civilized game a bit and say perhaps, "Look, if capitalism cannot integrate these people, it still must accept that these people have every right to exist, and that right trumps property laws." Even here there is a certain indignity to the so-called homeless, but even more so to those who pay rent. Not because the latter are more deserving because they work for their keep, but because they are fools who pay rent as though only in that way do they belong!

In other times, perhaps seemingly more brutal than ours, if you were driven away from where you were, you just moved somewhere else. And this gets us to my next point. It was without a doubt the agriculturists that made the world homeless, turned the wild and the free into a place of property and slavery.

---

23 John Locke, Two Treatises on Government, Book 2, (London: PRINTED MDCLXXXVIII), sections as noted above. http://www.johnlocke.net/two-treatises-of-government-book-ii/

John Zerzan & The Paleolithic

John Zerzan has written extensively on primitivism. His golden age, as it were, is that period where humans lived in small-uncivilized groups, hunter-gatherers, pre-iron age. This is really after Rousseau's ideal period of self-sufficiency, but the points are similar. Civilization has meant for Zerzan, as well, a great reduction of freedom and personal autonomy. Language, small social groups and even tools are fine, as long as specialization does not occur, and the groupings remain non-hierarchal. This period would have still maintained plenty of personal freedom and plenty of free time. When this period, which is many hundreds of thousands of years of our evolution, is taken into account, it is far more than the period of civilization, so it might be safe to say that these are our most ancient evolutionary predispositions that put us at odds with our current culture. That we are predisposed to idleness, wandering and autonomy would provide some basis for understanding our constant frustration and anxiety in our present state.

In his essay 'Future Primitive,' John Zerzan reviews the current anthropological literature and paints a distinctly un-Hobbesian picture of the uncivilized life. For the Palaeolithic period, which makes up the vast majority of the lifespan of our species, we were essentially foragers, not really hunters, more scavengers. There was no real sexual division of labour, almost no violence, and we lived a life requiring about two hours of 'work' a day. More dedicated hunting arose when we moved to colder and harsher climates.

Violence, hierarchy, and religion arose together with agriculture and the domestication of animals. In the wake of agriculture came disease, famine, property, long hours of work, the sexual division of labour, the priesthood, power, violence and war. We live in the wake of this horrendous transformation, lost, homeless. As long as this nightmare has been, it has not suppressed that memory we experience as a dream, of the time of the wild and the free. Zerzan writes:

> During the vast time-span of the Palaeolithic, there were remarkably few changes in technology (Rolland 1990). Innovation, "over 2 1/2 million years measured in stone tool development was practically nil," according to Gerhard Kraus (1990). Seen in the light of what we now know of prehistoric intelligence, such 'stagnation' is especially vexing to many social scientists. "It is difficult to comprehend such slow development," in the judgement of Wymer (1989). It strikes me as very plausible that intelligence, informed by the success and satisfaction of a gather-hunter existence, is the very reason for the pronounced absence of 'progress'. Division of labor, domestication, symbolic culture — these were evidently refused until very recently.[24]

24. John Zerzan, "Future Primitive," from *Future Primitive And Other Essays*, (New York: Autono-

In 'Future Primitive', Zerzan argues that the bloodthirsty Hobbesian 'all against all' never existed. (I might add that this is more our Hobbesian future, and our reality, than our primitive past.) More recent archaeological and anthropological studies direct us away from "a bloodthirsty, macho version of prehistory."[25] What does in fact mark our prehistory, the vast majority of the life of our species, millions of years rather tens of thousands, is primarily a foraging life. A life with no sexual division of labour, with food sharing, cooperation, little or no violence and a life without marked time, primarily one of leisure. We did not really 'hunt', we scavenged meat or caught fish by hand but our diet consisted primarily of fruit and vegetables[26]. We had little need for more than the basic cutting tools.

What brought on the anxiety and alienation which marks our current miserable existence was the domestication of animals and agriculture. With very few exceptions, all of our so-called 'primitive' or 'aboriginal' people are post-Palaeolithic. That Rousseau came to the same conclusion, well before even theories of evolution were solidified, is rather remarkable. It is, I think, because the source of our anxiety is a species memory of this time as the wild and the free. It is an evolutionary memory, perhaps, that forms our nascent consciousness when we are born or even prior.

Zerzan also refers to studies in brain-injured patients which conclude that language is not necessary to complex thought. This could also be true of infants. We do notice, with some surprise, the ability of a newborn horse to stand very soon after being born and that aboriginal tribes relate to their children in quite different ways than we the civilized[27]. I do not remember any moment in my life when I did not see myself as fully formed, despite what others might say to me. But civilization does infantilize us to the point that we never really grow up. I suspect this is down to the fact that we lack that kind of self-sufficiency that any other immature animal has. The current evidence shows us — and logic would

media, 1994), p 23.

25. ibid., p.17.

26. One recent phenomenon illustrates how deeply brain-washed we are by the story of our pre-history that developed while imperialism and slavery were in full swing is the so called Caveman or Palaeolithic diet. Because it suits the purposes of the rulers of 'civilization' to justify slavery, it also suits them to purvey the idea that the Caveman was a brute and that sexual division of labour was 'natural.' And so the fantasy of the male hunter and the female gatherer-nurturer is propped up as a relationship based on a naturalization of gender roles. So the Caveman hunts and eats meat, grunts, farts and demands sex as it suits him. The 'caveman diet,' as described, has a very high percentage of animal foods. The high amount of animal protein of the Palaeolithic people is a supposition that is not backed up by what we know. For instance, fishing did not become common until 35 or 40 thousand years ago and bows do not appear until 8000 BCE. As there was no agriculture we were primarily gatherers and given that our closest genetic cousins are higher apes, which are frugivores, we probably supplemented our diet with carrion, eggs and small prey.

27. For one thing, childhood ends much sooner. Modernism extends adolescence ever longer to the point where most Western men are not fully adult until they are 30. Whereas in aboriginal societies, self-sufficiency is expected in the early teens.

have to insist on it — that we would not have survived if we were not at some point in our evolution not only self-sufficient, but immensely knowledgeable of our environment and extremely efficient.

It is that necessary corollary to civilization, religion, that is the foundation of our infantilization. The cry from religionists is that modernity has created moral uncertainty. Moral certainty is however, the moral status of the indoctrinated child: 'ours is not to reason why…' Simon Critchley writes: "The problem of secularism, the problem of the secular world, is that we haven't achieved it yet. The problem of modernity is not that we have somehow got beyond modernity. On the contrary we haven't achieved modernity. Modernity would be the achievement of a secular form of life, and we haven't got there yet."[28] Critchley goes on to say: "Ethics are not handed to us on Sinai on large tablets; they are things we have to create for ourselves. We have to become grown-ups."[29]

In light of Zerzan's image of the self-sufficient human, which is very similar to Rousseau's natural man, we can now see that civilization and religion are not only co-extensive with our inability to survive by our wits, but major contributing factors to this disempowerment and its corollary, anxiety. Religion, in fact, removes responsibility from us, by teleporting ultimate consequences into the outer space of heaven and hell. Religion defers responsibility until final judgement and thus takes from us responsibility in a bought and paid for forgiveness. Religion is the first form of lifestyle advertisement, a theological 'Freedom 55.' It makes us perennial teenagers.

This infantilized culture with its endless adolescence involves not only lack of responsibility but also laziness. The whole commodity transaction culture plays to these lacks, or anxieties. Incompleteness is necessary for consumerism. Consumerism MUST create or enhance this sense of lack, the anxiety of missing something. We do not hold ourselves responsible for this state, for our loathsome pettiness, our inability to survive by our wits. What is made available to us, to counter our inabilities, is the time-saving gadget. The time-saving gadget will give us more time to use the time-wasting gadget (entertainment/art). Our responsibility is overshadowed by the masturbatory release of these purchases. But then buyers regret sets in, and we know the lack is still there.

If you won't do what I want you to do you are lazy. We are loathe to admit laziness and bristle when the insult is thrown our way. Our response is the flaccid 'you are not the boss of me!' The dynamic here is master-slave, slavery being the direct consequence of civilization. The slave is lazy because she won't do what the boss tells her to do. She is compelled to do so on pain of a beating, rape or death. (Such consequences will be rained down upon her in any case.) The slave will do

---

28. Simon Critchley, *Impossible Objects: Interviews*, (Cambridge: Polity Press, 2012), p 39.
29. ibid., p 39.

the slave's job because she wants to live. This is just one aspect made clear to us by Camus' *The Myth of Sisyphus*. Sisyphus chooses life. But slavery requires violence because the slave has a memory not only of freedom (because freedom in and of itself is useless) but of self-sufficiency. And our present day relative 'freedom' vis-à-vis the slave, is minor, as we are not only wage slaves but commodity prostitutes.

What is offered to us is the sole option of giving our time to someone else, the estate owner, the priest, the lord, the entrepreneur, and in return we get money to buy what we have made for the profit of others. It's a lousy deal and so, like any peasant, we always try to give less than is expected of us, to steal or sabotage what we are paid to do. We get together over drinks and complain about our asshole bosses. All of which only enhances our sense of this lack of self-sufficiency.

It is a natural response of the peasant who, only recently, in the last 25,000 years, has become enslaved to agriculture. This laziness works away at your self-respect and seems to put more space between us and that freedom of self-sufficiency. And it is only enhanced by the what-the-fuck attitude and the drunkenness that seems to accompany 'work' in all cultures, whether it is from alcohol or drugs.

In the Palaeolithic period our knowledge about our environment made us efficient. There was no need to work more than what was necessary. It wasn't laziness, it was intelligence. This combination of irresponsibility and so-called laziness is integrally related to this loss of self-respect that ends when we no longer can truly fend for ourselves. There is a fantasy about agriculture, that it can allow us to be self-sufficient or that it was like that at some point for homesteaders. But rent makes this impossible. And now, as control over agriculture is held by corporate power, it is impossible even to 'make a living' as we like to call the trade of time for money called 'work.' Even so, agriculture is a mug's game because by its very nature agriculture destroys soil. Its uniformity over acres creates a monoculture, and is unsustainable. Once the soil is destroyed it takes back breaking work to partially restore it. This is where slaves come in handy.

What Zerzan makes clear is that agriculture is already the end of self-sufficiency, but more emphatically, it is the beginning of slavery up to and including wage-slavery. Even as we know that the cattlemen are somewhat, and the Natives even more so, closer to the sense of self-sufficiency we crave, they are still enslaved to animal husbandry and/or agriculture in hierarchal gangs which breed violence and dependence. What they have that we don't have is a 'taste' of it, a hint of an idea that they can survive alone if need be.

Living with animals as food or beasts of burden has made us sick. By enslaving animals to life of drudgery we flood our system with disease. Most known diseases derive from this close interaction with animals.[30] Slavery of animals

30. "Thus, when the human population became sufficiently large and concentrated, we reached the stage in our history at which we could at least evolve and sustain crowd diseases confined to our own

probably inspired slavery of humans. So this is the holy trinity of civilization: agriculture, religion and slavery. It's hard at this point to know how cultivated grain's impact on our diet and health will eventually pan out, but it does certainly look as though, while grain can feed billions of us, it tends to make us fat and stupid. It seems to be linked with much modern disease.

One cultural image that evokes a kind of Rousseauian longing is the mountain man. It's an image that we associate with the Appalachians, a solitary kind of self-sufficient outlaw who makes Mountain Dew and shoots at folks who approach his area. The outlaw status of these bootleggers, like Popcorn Sutton, may be a sedentary version of Shane.

The ridiculously woeful movie *Jeremiah Johnson*, made in 1972, is a Hollywood auteur version of the mountain man. Considering the time it was made, one cannot miss the connection with hippie ideals. The protagonist comes west to escape the Mexican War. After some incompetent attempts that almost lead to his death he meets another mountain man who teaches him what to do. It is made clear that this master hermit has learned a great deal from the Natives about to how to survive alone in the Utah mountains. Johnson respects the Natives and eventually creates a family with a Native woman and child. He is forced by circumstance to traverse a Native burial ground and his family is killed as retribution.

The connection with draft dodgers, back to the land and the respect that hippies had for indigenous culture are reflected here. The movie leaves one with a sense of hopelessness reflecting perhaps the end of 60's idealism in its own rather ham-fisted way.

Del Gue: Which way you headed, Jeremiah?
Jeremiah Johnson: Canada, maybe. I hear there is land there a man has never seen.
Del Gue: Well, keep your nose in the wind, and your eyes along the skyline.
Jeremiah Johnson: I will do that, Del Gue.[31]

In 1972 it may have seemed possible to be somewhere beyond the law of property, where one could stop the madness.

---

species. ...Where did these diseases come from? ... Among animals, too, epidemic diseases require large, dense, populations and don't afflict just any animal: they're confined mainly to social animals... Hence when we domesticated social animals, such as cows and pigs, they were already afflicted by epidemic diseases just waiting to be transferred to us." Jared Diamond, *Guns Germs and Steel* (New York: W.W. Norton & Company, 1997) p. 206..
31. Dialogue from *Jeremiah Johnson* (Warner Bros, 1972). http://en.wikipedia.org/wiki/Jeremiah_Johnson_%28film%29

One thing I fear is that the reader will get the idea that what I and others like Zerzan seem to be saying is that everything was hunky dory. There would still have been death, pain, disappointment and worry. How I look at it is that if one knows one can survive by one's own hand, it relieves a basic anxiety which disarms certain psychological and emotional problems. Anxiety is a vague dread, It is dependent on a lack of self-sufficiency, i.e. I cannot survive without this job. I enjoy myself with a kind of dread, that this time of plenty may pass and I will be on the streets begging. One can imagine money running out, but one does not imagine self-sufficiency running out until one is very old.

In the 70s and 80s, sexual liberation moved from open and joyous acceptance to rigid identity politics. Amongst some neo-primitive literature there are propositions that sexual jealousy did not exist amongst Palaeolithic groups. I doubt this very much. Love is not a conditional emotion dependent on a rational calculation. Still, there is a sense that one can imagine, that sexual jealousy would be lessened because each person is capable of surviving on their own. Some sexual jealousy is caused because of a need for support in atomized modernity. The line in songs is, "I can't make it on my own." We all know that working hard does not guarantee one a job. And in the modern world, unless you come from the wealthy, this is a matter of luck not skill. Plenty of incompetent people fill jobs while the competent ones less willing to be compliant are without jobs. In the Palaeolithic world, exile does not mean death because one is self-sufficient. It is necessary to mate outside family groups. So there are forces that drive reconciliation and the relative plenty and ease of savannah life means there are few pressures.

I'd say that suggestions by neo-anarchists that new social structures have psycho-sexual benefits are leftovers from Reich and Marcuse. I don't throw these guys on the dustbin but sexual liberation is far trickier than what was imagined in the 20s and the 60s-80s. Identity politics blew this all up. As I said, there would be relief from certain sexual pressures in a new Palaeolithic life, but there still would be some problems. I don't necessarily think that polyandry would take hold. Whether couples stay together forever or have multiple partners is not clear. But I suspect that simultaneous polyandry is out of the question. Different partners over time might be more likely.

Sexual liberation is somewhat nonsensical unless you are specifically talking about recognition of homosexuality. The idea that everyone will become bi-sexual is nonsense. In the 80s there was a sense that this was required by some people. Mandatory bisexuality is just as oppressive as mandatory heterosexuality.

Trade is Evil
Distribution is Evil

The first person, who, having enclosing a plot of land, took it into his head to say *this is mine* and found people simple enough to believe him, was the true founder of civil society. What crimes, wars, murders, what miseries and horrors, would the human race been spared, had someone pulled up stakes or filled in the ditch and cried out to his fellow men: Do not listen to this imposter; you are lost. You are lost if you forget that the fruits of the earth belong to all, and the earth to no one!

—Jean-Jacques Rousseau, *Discourse on the Origin of Inequality*[32]

Agriculture does not work towards self-sufficiency, it works towards surplus. It is this surplus that makes religion possible. Surplus is not sharing, it is a means of taxation. Hence cometh the tithe. Shamans are the first to extract filthy lucre from the people who were once their equals. The priest exacts the tithe as a payment for divine favour. What more can you ask from a commodity than to contain a giant mythic lie. The shaman with his bones or sticks, drugs and wild get-up, is the first bait and switch, show and steal salesperson. The priest is the next phase, which pumps up the volume of this early version of brand loyalty marketing.

It has to take on that lust inducing air about itself, because it's taking the place of sharing. We all know that not having a smart-phone is a kind of isolationist hell. Having one though, is a communion with God, our salvation. If there was sharing and no surplus, we couldn't make this back alley exchange with our local pimp and there would be no transubstantiation of the soul. As Zerzan (quoting Kevin Duffy) has drawn our attention to (referencing the Mbuti Pygmies, until recently our closest example of what Palaeolithic was like,) the uncivilized life was marked by sharing.

"Try to imagine," he [Duffy] counsels, "a way of life where land, shelter, and food are free, and where there are no leaders, bosses, politics, organized crime, taxes or laws. Add to this the benefits of being part of a society where everything is shared where there are no rich people and no poor people, and where happiness does not mean the accumulation of material possessions."[33] The Mbuti have never domesticated animals or planted crops. There is no surplus value. There is no concept of abstract value earned by drudgery to be exchanged for guilty pleasures.[34]

---

32 op. cit., p. 60.
33. Zerzan, op.cit. p. 30 from Duffy, Kevin, *Children of the Forest (New York*: Dodd, Mead & Company, *1984)*
34. ibid., p. 30

And further to the same point, as Hole and Flannery (1963) summarized: "No group on earth has more leisure time than hunters and gatherers, who spend it primarily on games, conversation and relaxing."[35]

In light of this we can perhaps understand the resistance of the slave that has become known as laziness. If it was all that the slave and generations of slaves had ever known, it would seem to follow that this was their mere lot in life, that resistance was futile and that they would simply accept the order of things. While it may seem to veer into some sort metaphysical or quasi-mystical space to suggest this, perhaps there is a suppressed memory of self-sufficiency at the base of our anxieties and our resistance to completely accepting the trade-off of smart-phones for idleness and play. One feature of smart-phones is that they require doing a lot of crappy work to get them, not just going into the creepy store and talking to the pompous twat selling them, or the driving in traffic where people may consider killing you in order to get there 3.5 seconds earlier than you, or the oppressive and depressing atmosphere of the store, let alone the thought bubble over your head that says "sucker!" but most of all the many hours at your shitty job you do to pay the interest, maybe, on your maxed out credit card.

If we compare the Palaeolithic forager existence to the post agriculture one, we note that the former's world is not alien, it is immediately available to her. There is no deferment. Agriculture has already built into its process a theological component. One has to plant the seeds and work very hard for many months, and eventually the payoff. There is a very long deferment between need and satisfaction. The shaman offers up some malarkey about being able to intervene, to provide a kind of spiritual insurance for the crop yield if you just pay up. And of course if it all works out, everyone is happy and none the wiser. But if things don't work out it is always because the supplicant has failed in their duty, they have sinned and the god(s) are mad. However this works out, the shaman is always ahead, like the insurance agent. Pascal's wager, though really a declaration of atheism, is the same bad logic of insurance, necessitated by our isolation, that we have no tribe:

> Let us weigh the gain and the loss in wagering that God is. Let us estimate these two chances. If you gain, you gain all; if you lose, you lose nothing.

> —Blaise Pascal, *Pensées* part III, §233[36]

---

35. ibid., p. 31.

36. The wager is an inadvertent declaration of atheism because one cannot make that wager in 'good faith.' To 'take it on faith' is demanding an 'ask no questions' stance. To ask for the proof of God assumes his non-existence, it is *ipso facto* blasphemy. It is unlike the 'other minds problem,' because even if it is possible that everyone else is an automaton or a fantasy, it does not change that the existence of the question requires the questioner. Yes, essentially *cogito ergo sum*, which is also atheist, because consciousness does not presume a creator. The *reductio ad absurdum* cannot be "God exists therefore I do" nor can it be "I exist therefore God exists". The question, "How did I get here?" does

The wager we make is that things could be worse, so we stay with the evil we know.

With foraging, one understands what one needs and knows what to do to get it. There is no deferment. Our specific modernist bias views such people as primitive. In popular parlance they are little more than dumb apes. Zerzan reports that foragers often eat more than a hundred different species of plants. This not only shows a varied diet but a tremendous knowledge of their environment, not only do they eat one hundred different plants but they can distinguish them from hundreds of others.

In *The Harmless People* (1959), Marshall told how one Bushman walked unerringly to a spot in a vast plain, "with no bush or tree to mark the place," and pointed out a blade of grass with an almost invisible filament of vine around it. He had encountered it months before the rainy season when it was green. Now in parched weather, he dug there to expose a succulent root and quenched his thirst.[37]

Because it is presumed that agriculture is progress, it is also assumed that our predecessors had not yet evolved enough to have the intelligence for agriculture. This prejudice made the long Palaeolithic period rather baffling to anthropologists. Fire was around for two million, and the first tools were around for possibly three million years. The tools themselves did not multiply or improve much for the vast majority of that time. While this has tended to be explained by a species demarcation, based on an assumption of intelligence, recent work has shown that the tools available indicate intelligence equal to modern adults.

Why very little change then? Why indeed swap a way of life of immediate satisfaction of needs based on a few hours of work each day and the rest of one's time in play for one of 10-12 hour work days where the tenuous reward may or may not be realized until months later. It is a well known fact that the vast majority of human disease comes from interaction with animals and their domestication. This transition from a general easy-going life of gatherers to a miserable disease-ridden existence marked by class division and slavery was undoubtedly what anyone would want to avoid. Religion was both the catalyst for class and gender divisions of labour but also for slavery. God is the banker. The priest is his broker. Zerzan references Johannessen on the transition who "offers the thesis that resistance to the innovation of planting was overcome by the influence of shamans, among the Indians of the Southwest..."[38]

---

not require a God question.
37. Zerzan, op. cit., p.33.
38 ibid. p.38.

In this new scenario of our prehistory there is no Hobbesian nightmare. It undermines the normal polarities of the argument in political philosophy. As Carl Schmitt said, there are two traditions in political thought: authoritarian and anarchist. They both derive from conceptions of human nature. If you think human beings are wicked, you turn to an authoritarian conception of politics, the Hobbesian-Machiavellian-Straussian line. This will always be more attractive to intellectuals because they think of themselves as having deeper insight into human nature than others and it corresponds to the wickedness we intellectuals tend to see all over the place. If, in fact, any inherent wickedness is at least under suspicion with this new anthropology, and as we can see that humans are perfectly capable of non-hierarchical, non-violent cooperation without either law, religion or property, then the Hobbesian thread is exposed for the apologist obfuscation it really is.

As Raj Patel has argued in *The Value of Nothing*, there are some examples in our current situation which demonstrate that we can exist without the 'wealth of nations.' His example is the new indigenous movement, best exemplified by the Zapatista self-government which functions without elections, where everyone does a stint as a representative. The conditions built into their political structure foster cooperation and consensus.[39]

The question, however, will become whether (given our perennial state of financial and ecological collapse staved off only by constant deferment of pain through angels and demons of macroeconomic money policy) our future will be a post-apocalyptic Hobbesian nightmare or something akin to our Palaeolithic past. It is quite clear that macro-agriculture will destroy our source of food if various forms of the toxic war against nature don't. It's hard to know if, in the immediate future, foraging will be possible, let alone a somewhat more benevolent form of agriculture. Such a thing remains a question. Can we have agriculture without slavery and soil destruction?

It seems to me, on the face of it, unlikely that foraging can sustain 7 billion people. Agriculture will certainly not be able to sustain this population much longer, since it's not clear it's sustaining us now. Any aware person realizes that we are close to so many ecological and economic tipping points that we will have to come to realize that while the Hobbesian nightmare is not our past, it may very likely be our future. The invisible hand has certainly increased wealth but it is not a high tide lifting all boats; most of us are not in even in boats but are drowning in the water.

---

39. For a detailed description of Zapatista governance see Raj Patel, *The Value of Nothing* (Toronto: HarperCollins, 2009), pp. 179-186.

Hippies and Diggers

'Commons' is an Old English word. According to my Japanese friends, it is quite close to the meaning that *iriai* still has in Japanese. 'Commons,' like *iriai*, is a word which, in pre-industrial times, was used to designate certain aspects of the environment. People called commons those parts of the environment for which customary law exacted specific forms of community respect. People called commons that part of the environment which lay beyond their own thresholds and outside of their own possessions, to which, however, they had recognized claims of usage, not to produce commodities but to provide for the subsistence of their households. The customary law which humanized the environment by establishing the commons was usually unwritten. It was unwritten law not only because people did not care to write it down, but because what it protected was a reality much too complex to fit into paragraphs. The law of the commons regulates the right of way, the right to fish and to hunt, to graze, and to collect wood or medicinal plants in the forest.

—Ivan Illich, *Silence As A Commons*[40]

To understand the commons today, it's worth starting in feudal England—the birthplace of modern capitalism—by looking at the Magna Carta's twin charter, the Charter of the Forest. Although largely forgotten today, the Charter of the Forest guaranteed the ability of commoners to access pasture for their animals, to till land, to collect wood, harvest honey, use medicinal plants, forage and so on. …a commons right guaranteed freedoms over local resources for everyone.[41]

— Raj Patel, *The Value of Nothing*

The original Diggers took the bold move of planting their crops on land which had been seized in the Enclosures. Although their mode of subsistence was agriculture they attacked the idea of homelessness not landlessness. The solution wasn't to own land, but to see it as something that should not and could not be owned. It was an early form of class warfare.

It was, by an historical perspective, seen as a step backward. Even for Marx this stage marked by the enclosures and affirmation of private property was necessary for the amassing of wealth that made the engine of capitalism possible. For Marx, the brutalism of capitalism was a necessary step in the creation of techniques and wealth that would allow for the transition to communism, "From each according to his ability, to each according to his need."

40. http://www.preservenet.com/theory/Illich/Silence.html
41. Raj Patel, op. cit., pp. 98-99.

So while the Diggers avowed something like a primitive communism, they were standing in the way of real communism from Marx's perspective. I think though, Rousseau saw the future in the rear view mirror, to use a McLuhanesque formulation. The question of the inevitability of the modern is always presumed in our discussions. When we talk about these moments of desire for the wild and the free, they are bracketed as a kind of wistful dreaming for something that cannot be. To return to the Palaeolithic is absurd, crazy, and insane.

The Diggers of the Haight-Ashbury in the 60s were in a similar position, except they embraced the notion that their ideas were absurd, crazy and insane. They, like the Diggers of old, wanted something of a modification of the current state of affairs rather than its complete overturning. They did use tactics to undermine certain core aspects of the modern: rent, money and consumerism. Their free store was an especially poignant absurdity, a moment of Dada politics.

Maintaining the concept of 'free' as a central tenet for the San Francisco Diggers — there were also 'free stores' in Vancouver and in New York run by Yippies, and the Provos in Amsterdam did similar things — but it is something, in the totalizing context of modern capitalism, that requires a lot of energy and money. Even if one is using squats there are always costs, not just in time. Squatting and panhandling, while removing one at least partially from some aspects of the normal money economy, are within that urban setting not only taxing but demeaning.

The next step then, it seems, was the back to the land commune. Not only to get out of the money economy but off the grid as well. It is again this desire to achieve sustainability, to live by one's own hand.

All the religious sects who came to America to escape persecution must have accepted, even if their theology did not, the right of other religions to coexist in the same civil society. And in recognizing this they implicitly accepted the concept of a non-theocratic state, even if America never fully escaped theocratic elements. This meant that there was a civil space that was neutral and secular. Religion was in another sphere. It is more the idea of America than the reality of America that is important here. It is very related to the idea of the Wild West (the wild and the free) that we talk about when we discuss *Shane* and the Western. It is a thought experiment about the future of life that parallels Rousseau's thought experiment of a pre-historical human.

The initial solution was a kind of keeping to one's own, allowing separate societies to coexist. It informs the American idea of federalism. Even today there are many remnants of these original groups who live in some ways outside, while technically inside, the USA. One consequent overriding idea for these communities is autonomy. This autonomy for a closed religious sect living self-contained lives is mirrored in the free-rangers. The self-contained community wants also to be free of the law, so outlaw in this sense, but unlike the free-rangers, with their own separate law.

While very old communities like the Amish continue to exist in the USA, many new ones have risen up. None were so related to the theme of this essay as the hippie back-to-the-land communalists. There is no stereotype from the 60s more maligned than hippies and communalists though they come from a very old European and American tradition. While some hippy communes became homes of drug-induced lassitude and others were religious crackpots, there were many whose main priorities were ecological and anti-commercial. The idea that was strongly advocated by them, that goes back to Rousseau, was self-sufficiency. The ideas of 1) getting off the grid and 2) opting out of the money economy, are related to the concept of personal freedom that Rousseau saw as existing prior to civilization.

It was obvious to the hippies that rent, for example, obliged one to participate through employment or other activity in a kind of exchange that either nullified or severely restrained one's personal autonomy. Communes within the city, while affording a certain autonomy from social mores, still obliged one to operate to a degree in the money economy, even when in squats. The back to the land commune was the next step to move away from the money economy and towards self-sufficiency.

The reason for the happiness of the noble savage is freedom, for one, and the satisfaction of knowing one can survive by one's own wits, for another. Autonomy and independence are keys to this. Rousseau's noble savage is more the fully self-sufficient natural man loner, but the hippie is striving to maintain self-sufficiency as a group effort. The hippie commune is a society. More than Rousseau's noble savage it is a case of Kropotkin-like mutual aid. The interpersonal and/or social aspect was the downfall of most communes. Many ideals like free love or children raised in an extended family often ended up causing friction with people leaving on their own or expelled. Hierarchies arose or equality was destroyed in squabbling. Yet many communes did in fact survive these trials.

Nevertheless, some of the ideas of the hippie commune are now really core to the ecological movement and seem ever more relevant given the unpredictable threats such as oil shortage and global warming. Getting off the grid has far more resonance now as inconceivable as it may seem to many. It is rather ironic that the generation that brought these ideas again to the fore, resurrected from Thoreau and Rousseau, have driven us to the brink of disaster in a frenzy of hyper-consumption. We just cannot think of enough ways to consume more and more energy in a circus of throwaway consumer items.

"*I saw coming towards the house a kind of vehicle drawn like a sledge by four yahoos*"

Pessimism and Anti-Utopia

I have been assured by a very knowing American of my acquaintance in London, that a young healthy child well nursed is at a year old a most delicious, nourishing, and wholesome food, whether stewed, roasted, baked, or boiled; and I make no doubt that it will equally serve in a fricassee or a ragout.

— Jonathan Swift, *A Modest Proposal*

Literary utopias are critiques of a current state of affairs. Swift's *Gulliver Travels* is a satire of the utopian urge. It reflects the implied disputes between Hobbes' government as a defence against the brutal all against all versus Thomas More's *Utopia* or Samuel Butler's *Erewhon*. Swift's satire is hard to pin down. The travels are a search for an answer, like Columbus or Marco Polo, in the distant lands. There seems to be disappointment everywhere.

Gulliver Travels ends with spoiled utopia. The horses, houyhnhnms, have noble dignity while humans (Yahoos) are brutish and mired in their own shit. The houyhnhnms could be seen as a prior superior animal with consciousness before the fall. Houyhnhnms have the dignity of Rousseau's natural man. I wouldn't be the first to suggest that *Gulliver's Travels* may be a critique of Hobbes. Hobbes also sees people as potentially Yahoos who require the body politic to be reined in. The unruliness, Hobbes is saying requires state power, is in fact referring to the English Revolution and the Diggers and Levellers.

Is there any more damning text of civilization than Swift's *A Modest Proposal*? If some sort of police state, as in the monarchy, the constitutional executive or Stalinist cult of personality, is what holds us back from all against all, other utilitarian calculations such as infants as a food source make sense despite our squeamishness. These calculations are regularly inflicted on the dispossessed in Africa so we can have cell phones. They would have starved anyway, they might as well live a short brutal life providing utility for others.

For me, any future utopia must look backwards to something more primitive. All future oriented utopias are dystopias. Terry Eagleton gave a lecture about Marx and Theodicy at York University in 2010[42]. Briefly, theodicy is historically a response to the problem of evil for Christianity: Why do bad things happen to good people?" and "Why do bad people succeed?" Theodicy is a kind of rationalization for the misery of the world while God sits idly by having the power to change it. As omnipotent God could theoretically ensure that good people succeed

---

42. Big Ideas: Terry Eagleton on Marxism as a Theodicy. http://ww3.tvo.org/video/165511/terry-eagleton-marxism-theodicy or http://podcasts.tvo.org//bi/audio/007550_48k.mp3

and are happy, and bad people fail and are unhappy. This is clearly not the case. God then is the source for the evil, or he sees it as proper.

Arguments put forward by theologians to explain this are what is called theodicy. Augustine argues that good and evil came into the world through the original sin. The existence of current evils are punishment for that original sin. Alternately, our only ability to achieve goodness was to freely choose it, thus requiring free will, meaning the ability to do other than the good. And so, evil exists because of us and we must overcome it.

Now in this world we are in a weird moral game, where the deck is stacked against us, and God is shown to be willing to toy with us to test our mettle. We look at Abraham, whose son God has asked for in sacrifice. In the end God relents but what, pray tell, was the point? God knew what would happen. As in Job, God seems like a little boy more willing to take a fly, pluck off some of its wings, or pull a limb off a grasshopper and watch it suffer with a kind of bemusement. Levinas, interestingly enough, argues that theodicy is blasphemous and the source of all immorality, whether god or profit is invoked it is fundamentally evil: Jules Simon describes Levinas position here:

In fact, in the presence of innocent suffering, the ethical response should invoke absence and the very loss of possibility. Such an invoking of absence and an uncertain horizon attends to an irrecoverable past inflected with the voices of those who should have been heard but whose voices have been either violently silenced or indifferently ignored. But even such simple testimony to lost and absent others is insufficient because such testimony is just a preliminary response in the presence of the suffering of innocent ones. What this means is that it is not enough to point toward those who have suffered, toward the loss of new beginnings and children. Those very children are victims of institutional structures that support the actions of those members of our society who have lost their sense of responsibility. Thus, the creation of an environment where the voice of the victim can be raised as narrative testimony needs to be accompanied by an ethical critique. Such a critique assesses the logical principles, presuppositions, and intentions of the policy makers and educators who instruct, influence, direct, and lead the many among us who cause suffering through direct intentions, complicit toleration, or indifferent complacency.[43]

Theodicy argues that there is some utility in evil, perhaps as a spur to strive for good. One must pass through the dark night of the soul in order to see the

---

43. Jules Simon, "Making Ethical Sense of Useless Suffering with Levinas." http://works.bepress.com/cgi/viewcontent.cgi?article=1003&context=julesimon

light. In other words, this means that pain and suffering are necessary for heaven. Marx felt the brutality of capitalism, however nasty and destructive, was a necessary step in order to get to socialism. On the other side though, communism supposedly does away with the state and we move, "From each according to his ability, to each according to his need".

This is theodicy but the goal of true communism would seem to imply something like anarchism. My problem with revolution is that it becomes inert, paralyzed by the militarism and paranoia that got it into power in the first place. And then what? They don't know what to do. You end up, as we now know, with state capitalism and extreme repression, ending either in the Chinese corporate state or the Russian Mafia economy. The West played no little part in this final result.

One of the academy's new heroes is mister theodicy himself, none other than you-need-to-crack heads-to-make-an-omelette Slavoj Žižek. Žižek, despite thousands of pages of endless blather in his books, is basically refried Lenin. State party dictatorship of the proletariat, violent overthrow or nothing. Every other action is basically worthless. This may have been possible in the early twentieth century, integrated lines of power and near total surveillance make revolution extremely unlikely, especially in the West where we are all amusing ourselves. He may be right about the impossibility of change but he is also ludicrously wrong about revolution. Revolution is no longer a political option it is merely a marketing technique.[44] Žižek's advice is, 'sit on your fat ass and watch TV until a *true* neo-Leninist party is formed.'

I am not talking about utopia per se. I am just talking about simple self-sufficiency. We all know we can do it but we don't. It is not progress or revolutionary. It might be post-apocalyptic. It is unlike *The Road* or *Mad Max*, Immediately in post-apocalyptic movies, we become gangs, the Hobbesian all against all. But why participate in this violence when there is nothing to gain, I mean there is no infrastructure so why bother seizing territory or oil and ruling like a Mafia boss? To achieve what? This is the fundamental problem with Hobbes' all against all: what will motivate and sustain this? Without our father, God or the king why will we just rip each other to shreds? Is it really laws and police that keep us from killing each other and stealing, looting and raping?

This is the common assumption;, that no state equals open gang violence. We've got Hobbes nightmare until Shane comes along. The options in *Shane* are artificially abrogated by the assumptions of civilization. I mean Natives are primarily bloodthirsty in the Western, they must kill and rape, so the Sheriff rides into town and cleans things up for business.

Let's put it this way, utopia as a construct is a pure negation, it is empty or vague, a la Marx. This is because we cannot imagine a world without a state,

44. For a devastating critique of Žižek's stance see Simon Critchley's *The Faith of the Faithless: Experiments in Political Theology* (London: Verso, 2012), especially pp. 227-237. If you would like a good soporific I can recommend Žižeks *Living In The End Times* (London: Verso, 2011).

or we are told it is unimaginable. You need Daddy around to smack some sense into people. So with Rousseau and Zerzan we have another idea. We were once not violent, there was no all against all, no situation of constant terror where everything was only resolved once we had a boss, the police and jails. Anarchism argues this, that authority and threats of violence are not necessities. The animal world is not all against all. Sure, lions chase and kill zebras but not wholesale. They only kill when they need to. In Hobbes, everyone is in Dante's hell eating each other over and over again without end. What is this idea except an argument for greater policing and surveillance?!

So one of our futures is our past, but the most current future is eco-apocalypse. Maybe the latter is necessary for the former but I don't see why, i.e. eco-collapse must come before neo-primitivism. This is where I think the hippies were right. They were wrong about agriculture, but right about opting out. Maybe there is a transition from subsistence farming to becoming gatherers. I don't know.

The first thesis of this book is: we are capable of self-sufficiency. And then, from there, that we can live in groups of shared self-sufficiency. If we couldn't do that we would have never survived for the hundreds of thousands of years we were human or the several million that we were sub-human.

Why would we assume that utopia is ever possible, is ever more than a way of identifying the elements of life that were lost or could be better than what we know? Life will always contain some good and bad as it does for all living things and our expectation of something more than that leads us to unhappiness, but this is not a reason not to strive for something more. In an ancient hunter-gatherer society a toothache could lead to a life of misery and death. I am pretty sure this wasn't anything more than an extremely rare occurrence. There were no refined sugars, no wheat, and no cultivated carbs. But shorter lives and possible death is not primarily a feature of ancient people. Even in mainstream anthropology they talk about the absence of most major diseases. Practically every serious ailment is derived from living with animals. Life expectancy was still shorter for sure. One might consider that long lives are not necessarily a good thing. First of all there is a greater use of resources but secondly, for the large majority of us, we are just extending our misery. To live 30 or 40 years in freedom might be a far better than 60 years of wage slavery in the so-called developed world that requires wretched misery and real slavery for most of the rest of the planet. To reiterate, we are the direct cause of this misery.

In some sense, the procession of humanity for all its evils has also brought improvements. It becomes a cost-benefit analysis. Some utopias – e.g. heaven – are calls to submit to authoritarian misery, so there is a reason to be suspicious of utopian ideas except for the principles they afford in the here and now. The essential humiliation is to become intellectually colonized and give up any possibility of independence. This is civilization's sales pitch. It is buyer's remorse again. The shamans sold us a scam and we are ashamed to admit it, so we just say, yeah it had to happen. And with this the shaman, the first priest con-man, we begin "humiliation as a life-style." If you are self-sufficient, you are confident, you don't need anything from anybody. This does not mean rugged individualism. Rugged individualism is shot through with resentment. I mean lots of us identify with the sentiment we see in the movies of *Dirty Harry,* "you assholes, you can all just go and fuck yourself for all I care!" We instinctively want to shout "yeah," but this is a puerile adolescent fantasy of self-sufficiency. If we can kick someone's ass then we can establish our worth. It just uncovers an aching hole of resentment and self-pity. So I would argue against that cost-benefit analysis as hucksterism. I can take being humiliated everyday by the Yahoos at work because you know they pay me x amount of bucks, and my pointless whining about it, which may include gestures of defiance, is just emblematic of my cowardice and impotence.

You cannot communicate to a multitude and a multitude cannot communicate with you. And the multitude might only be a hundred people. And your friends cannot be your audience. And audience cannot really be connected to you. I cannot listen to music by people who are my friends and really be a listener. I already like the person. So in the 'band,' the small group, you can get a kind of happy interchange. If you can be satisfied with that, like we once were, then we don't need a multitude. The multitude is a completely empty abstract; it is the nothingness. Yeah, I am going after the so-called post-Marxists Hardt and Negri and their corporate wet dream *Empire* : "The creative forces of the multitude that sustain Empire are also capable of autonomously constructing a counter-Empire, an alternative political organization of global flows and exchanges."[45] This was Mark Zuckerberg's bedtime story. Sorry guys, the Empire just keeps sucking up your flows and turning them into commodities. It's intuitive!

I like the anonymity that a large populace affords one, or at least I used to. I also sometimes know that people I don't know very well may respond more enthusiastically to something I make than people who know me well. Fewer surprises for the latter. Still I think humans are better in small groups. It is very hard not to see the massification of cities as an imposition, an affront. You feel this when driving and you get annoyed at people who slow you down.

That's why this book ends up in the crackpot territory. On one hand I see survival as us tied up with being less fruitful, i.e. there being fewer of us, and those fewer of us existing in smaller groups. And I see civilization as an unsolvable problem. Democracy is a kind of joke. I don't really believe that 29 million people have some right over me.

So much of this comes down to old saws and silly sayings. "You're not the boss of me!" Civilization and democracy have this one tenet as their basis,

---

45. Antonio Negri and Michael Hardt. *Empire.* (Cambridge: Harvard University Press. 2000). p. 15. Add Žižek and you get The Three Stooges of Post-Modernism.

"no opting out!" or perhaps "you can run but you can't hide." The arm of the state is long, and it will always find you in contempt and there will be a public shaming.

I am not sure that this book is hopeful, really it is hope-less. The only too expected criticism of it would be, if someone cared to comment, that this is utopian nonsense, you can't turn the clock back. And they may be right, the genie is out of the bottle. But that to me is far more pessimistic. On the one hand cynicism is ever popular, most people immediately reject any notion of change as ridiculous. Is it lack of imagination or just the sangfroid beaten into people by endless disappointment? Better to be a pessimist and be occasionally surprised than an optimist and shattered on a daily basis.

Even in those eco-utopias on the Ted Talks website one can't help but feel claustrophobic, they are so totalizing, and so 'engineered.' I am not sure this just ain't more Le Corbusier and there is nothing more dead or deadening than a Corbusier environment. Munch's *Scream* is made for just such environments. It's what I see in my mind when I think of the TD Centre in Toronto. It's just dreadfully dead and dour and pathetically hopeless, like the Pyramids. Monumentalism, which in its Christian Gothic form is meant to inspire, is really just a kind of stark emptiness; vast vaults of despair, screaming with a kind of endless anxiety

I know I was once loved without limit by my mother. But when I was loved so deeply I was pretty much a part of her, and almost nothing more. That happiness was a kind of moment where I was in a proto-conscious state, almost me, and almost aware of my happiness and the more I became me, the more estranged I was from my mother, the more anxious and unhappy I became. And so this architecture and culture is fundamentally an expression of this loss.

The closest that humans got to that experience was before civilization. When we were subhuman we probably had our most happy lives.

WILD WEST

WEEKLY

A MAGAZINE CONTAINING STORIES, SKETCHES Etc. OF WESTERN LIFE.

Issued Weekly—By Subscription $2.50 per Year.   Copyright, 1908, by Frank Tousey, Publisher, 24 Union Square, New York.

No. 284.   NEW YORK, MARCH 27, 1908.   Price 5 Cents.

YOUNG WILD WEST and "SILVER STREAM"; OR, THE WHITE GIRL CAPTIVE OF THE SIOUX.

By AN OLD SCOUT.

As Wild felled one of the redskins by a blow from the butt of his revolver, and sprang for the one with the tomahawk, the chief's daughter suddenly appeared. Raising her hands, she exclaimed: "Go back, Young Wild West. I will save her!"

The Pursuit of Things and the Reality of Misery

Columbia grows tulips for Holland and roses for Germany. Dutch companies send tulip bulbs and German companies send rose seedlings to immense plantations on the savannah of Bogotá. When the flowers are ready, Holland gets the tulips, Germany gets the roses, and Columbia gets low wages, damaged land, poisoned water. Thanks to these floral arrangements of the industrial era, the savannah is drying out and sinking, while the workers, nearly all of them women and children, are bombarded by pesticides and chemical fertilizers.

—Eduardo Galeano, *Upside Down: A Primer for the Looking Glass World* [46]

What do you want to be when you grow up?" Why is this a stupid question? Is being alive, being something? Why can't you just be? Why don't you leave me be? In the primitive, there is no being something, there is just being. They don't have to ask what they want to be when they grow up, because they don't grow up, they are always being.

There are many lies in the plan to be something. There are some folks, it seems, who follow a path to become a teacher or a doctor and become one as it were. And even these people will experience a kind of buyer's regret. Even a vocation is a job, you are tied down. You can't just be, you need to work, and the vocation is still work. Even the so-called creative artist, somewhat emblematic of a kind of personal freedom for many, makes work. Works of art are commodities to be bought and sold.

Why exactly do we ask the question? A zebra has no question of being something. If I try to be a writer like I am doing now, and failing miserably like I am doing now, or if I am succeeding gloriously like some latter day Milton, am I at rest, free of anxiety? Milton is always trying desperately to be Milton. That we admire Milton does little to settle his restlessness.

Even after I paint my masterpiece, then what? Am I staring at the masterpiece and thinking, well I guess I am 'someone.' Do we stop for a moment and think about how ridiculous this question is? Heidegger's question of being or Kant's or Sartre's, does any of it make the slightest sense beyond an elaborate game to escape the very question they are trying to answer.

Even "I am" seems to beg the question: "What are you?" Isn't the question of being some sort of attempt to quash the anxiety of its own inanity. The distance we are from self-sufficiency is the measure of our anxiety. If you know how to live independently there is no question of being.

46. *Upside Down: A Primer for the Looking Glass World,* (New York: Picador, 1998). p. 223.

There is a kernel of truth in Heidegger's idea of 'thrown-ness.' It speaks to the fact that there is no reason for us, no reason that we have become a plague upon ourselves and the earth. That we just "are" with no explanations is an excruciating fact. The unbearable pointlessness to our lives is combined with an ability to wreak untold misery on ourselves and everybody else. We are not the height of evolution, we are its demise, its death. We are the species that will destroy most if not all other species.

It is exemplary of our unlimited vanity to suppose that we have a purpose. There is no good, no utility, no point to us. We are, in fact, the very opposite of life, we are an infection, a disease, a plague of locusts. Consciousness is a deadly disease in our post-neolithic state. We are the primary disease. Other processes of decay, in animals and plants, work to recycle elements necessary for further life. We, on the other hand, poison, pollute and destroy in such a fashion that there is no recovery. We are the dead zone.

Agriculture was the first weapon of mass destruction, turning fertile land into deserts. If there is, in us, an irresistible impulse to agriculture and therefore hierarchy, class and violence, then there is no hope. If we are flexible enough to change our impulse to art, luxury and wealth, then perhaps there is a chance.

All of our current culture, even the oppositional elements, would indicate otherwise. It is the vanity of vanities that presides in the Twitter-verse and Facebook. For every witty comment or small insight there is a plethora of self-hatred. The idea of crowd-sourcing seems on the face of it a resurgence, a romantic ideal, like the possibility of some kind of uprising. The crowd is always that dysfunctional seething mass one encounters in Manhattan. We don't really move properly together in the crowd, everyone else is an impediment to us getting where we want to go, which is nowhere. There is no possibility of democracy in a crowd. The crowd is a growing infection.

The crowd is, itself, the fundamental requirement of that ponzi scheme we call capitalism. The ponzi scheme requires a steady stream of suckers, so at some point the predatory venture scam artist (or capitalist, same thing) can take your money and run. All the losers, with their useless vouchers, go home and lick their wounds. A short reprieve of buyer's guilt and self-pity before the next crowd-source scheme or ponzi comes along. Most everyone buys into, say, the smart phone (ironic name as usual[47]) as the new source of happiness, at least until

---

47. We know that the term 'smart phone,' while it seems to say that the phone is 'smart' is really a very typical sort of flattery to the buyer. Hey she's got a smart phone, she must be smart! The thing is, the phone itself is 'dumb.' It is inert. It is the antithesis of intelligence. It can only do what it was programmed to do, even if that means a meta process, where someone (a person, not another smart phone) programs it to do something new, it's the programmer that does this, not the phone. And there are demeaning aspects to owning a smart phone as it is given the task to do things for you, which you fail to do yourself, like remember your appointment. It is the shadow cast by your gullibility. Is the phone being smart or are you a sucker? And you don't just buy it, it is the gift that keeps on charging

it becomes a useless piece of junk.

They are then bulldozed by the ton into containers, sent off to China where our slaves can cook them in the streets for precious metals. Their misery, the inevitable cancer that will make their lives even more miserable is us. Just as we are with them at the end of the cycle, we are there at the beginning. We are in the mines in Africa, cracking the whip at slaves digging up that same precious metal being paid for in disease and hunger. They live in the festering toxic waste dump that most mines become, new dead zones, polluting for millennia. These people (for us they don't exist except in commercials and documentaries we can't distinguish from Iron Man) are the Untouchables of the modern world, cleaning up our shit. They are invisible to us. The crowd of the modern world has given these toxic dumps as our gift to the world. It is the gift that keeps on killing.

In the Preface to this little book, I referred to what I was writing as 'crackpot.' What is fundamental to being a crackpot is pessimism, but technological pessimism in particular. Technological optimism is a kind of plague. The question is never: "Should you make it?" It is only: "Can you make it?" No one ever asks if we really need to have 72 inch screens and computers in our pockets, it's just a race to who can get it to market the fastest. If the end result of LCD/LED technologies is billions of tons of toxic waste, it really doesn't matter, it's not relevant. Who cares! If we can turn sludge into fuel, we just do it. We are not concerned if this means we build a vast dead zone which will go on poisoning us for millennia. It's not relevant.

Pretty much all mining, and gas and oil production, create, for all intents and purposes, vast death, and from our perspective as human animals, permanent sources of toxicity, mutation and illness across all species not just ourselves. That we pay little heed to the misery down the street is despicable, but human. That we pay little heed to these other acres of ecological and personal misery we create 1000s of miles from us just shows how tiny our minds are, how petty our concerns, how limited our empathy is, how much decoration our ideas of morality are. Humanity is filthy scum, a virulent self-destructive pestilence that has infected every corner of the world with its shit and poisonous creations. We are vile and stupid creatures and the fact that we hold tight to insane technological optimism is delusional and repugnant.

It is unfortunate but true that the vast mob of gimme gimme people will never hear nor understand Rachel Carson. For example, if someone can profit by it then we do it, whatever petty and unnecessary pleasure it brings. Sourpuss crackpots like myself are just ignored as annoying whinging idiots. Technological

---

you, to remind you of that dentist appointment or making you available to everyone constantly. So you stare it while walking across the street and you get hit by a 'smart' car. Think again of *Gulliver's Travels*, the humans are up in the trees, covered in their own shit, and the horses, the former beasts of burden (animals as technology) are running the place. Erewhon indeed!

pessimists are just in the way. To the constant, "I want it!" the person who asks, "Why do you want it? Do you need it?" is a party pooper. I am raining on the parade. From my crackpot perspective it's hard not to see what is happening in the 'western world' as lemmings running off a cliff gleefully, credit cards to the max, texting on the latest device: "Hey come and join us, we are all running off a cliff, don't worry, everyone is doing it."

It is at this point, when I think about my arguments, party-pooping as they are, that I feel silly. It seems silly to point out to people who are running off a cliff with their eyes open, that they are running off a cliff and I think it will be bad in the end. It might even hurt. Am I missing something? I am running along with you, because I can't quite find a way off, being surrounded by this huge crowd all running, Where's the exit? I am not sure that if I could find a little place somewhere away from all these people running and just sit down that it would matter, I may just slide off the cliff anyways. I can't really sit still because the ground is moving beneath me and I'm done for like the rest of you.

Bibliography

• Alain Badiou, *Metapolitics* (London: Verso, 2005)

• Albert Camus, *Myth of Sisyphus.* http://www.sccs.swarthmore.edu/users/00/pwillen1/lit/msysip.htm

• Simon Critchley, *Infinitely Demanding: Ethics of Commitment, Politics of Resistance* (London: Verso, 2008)

• Simon Critchley, *How to Stop Living and Start Worrying* (Cambridge: Polity, 2010)

• Simon Critchley, *Impossible Objects: Interviews,* (Cambridge: Polity Press, 2012)

• Simon Critchley, *The Faith of the Faithless: Experiments in Political Theology* (London: Verso, 2012)

• Drew M. Dalton, *Longing for the Other: Levinas and Metaphysical Desire* (Pittsburgh: Duquesne University Press, 2009)

• Guy Debord. *Panegyric: volumes 1 & 2* (London: Verso, 2004)

• Jared Diamond, *Guns Germs and Steel* (New Yrok: W.W. Norton & Company, 1997)

• Terry Eagleton, *Trouble With Strangers: A Study of Ethics* (Chichester: Wiley-Blackwell, 2009)

• Eduardo Galeano, *Upside Down: A Primer for the Looking Glass World* (New York: Picador, 1998)

• Jean Genet, *Our Lady of the Flowers* (New York: Grove Press, 1963)

• David Hecht & Simone Maliqalim, *Invisible Governance: The Art of African Micropolitics* (Brooklyn: Autonomedia, 1994).

• Thomas Hobbes, *Leviathan* (London: Andrew Crooke, 1651). http://www.gutenberg.org/files/3207/3207-h/3207-h.htm

- The Invisible Committee, *The Coming Insurrection* (Los Angeles: Semiotext(e), 2009)

- John Locke, *Second Treatise of Government* (Indianapolis: Hackett, 1987)

- Naylor, R. T. *Crass Struggle: Greed, Glitz, and Gluttony in a Wanna-Have World* (Montreal & Kingston: McGill-Queens, 2011)

- Antonio Negri and Michael Hardt, *Empire.* (Cambridge: Harvard University Press, 2000)

- Sean O'Callaghan, *The Informer* (Toronto: Bantam Press, 1998)

- Raj Patel, *The Value of Nothing* (Toronto: Harper Perennial, 2009)

- Karl Polanyi, The *Great Transformation*, (Boston: Beacon Press, 1944)

- Jean-Jacques Rousseau, *The Basic Political Writings* (Indianapolis: Hackett, 1980)

- Gilles Slade, *Made to Break: Technology and Obsolescence in America* (New York: Prometheus Press, 2012)

- Gilles Slade, *The Big Disconnect: The Story of Technology and Loneliness* (Cambridge: Harvard University Press, 2006)

- Jean-Paul Sartre, *Saint Genet: Actor and Martyr* (George Brazilier, 1963)

- Tuck, Richard, *Hobbes, A Very Short Introduction* (Oxford: Oxford University Press, 1989)

- Raoul Vaneigem, *A Declaration of the Rights of Human Beings* (London: Pluto Press, 2003)

- Raoul Vaneigem, *The Movement of the Free Spirit* (New York: Zone Books, 1998)

- Peter Wollen, *Paris Manhattan: Writings on Art* (London: Verso 2004)

- Slavoj Žižek *Living In The End Times* (London: Verso, 2011).

- John Zerzan, *Elements of Refusal* (Seattle: Left Bank Books, 1988)

• John Zerzan, *Future Primitive And Other Essays*, (New York: Autonomedia, 1994),

• Alenka Zupancic, *Ethics of The Real: Kant,* Lacan (London: Verso, 2000)

Thanks to Rod Dubey for support, criticism and editing

Illustrations

- Front Cover & Frontispiece: "The Cow Boy" / J.C.H. Grabill, photographer, Sturgis, Dakota Ter. c1888. Library of Congress. http://commons.wikimedia. org/wiki/File:The_Cow_Boy_1888.jpg

- p. 6 Buffalo Bill's Wild West, 1890, Royale Photographie, Vuillemenot Montabone 188 Via Nazionale – Roma (Italia), http://commons.wikimedia. org/wiki/File:Buffalo_Bills_Wild_West_Show,_1890.jpg

- p. 8 TVA School-Village #1, Fifth Graders playing Pioneers and Indians, Tennessee Valley Authority. Information Office. 1937. http://commons. wikimedia.org/wiki/File:TVA_School-Village_%5E1,_Fifth_Graders_playing_Pioneers_and_Indians_-_NARA_-_280000.jpg

- p. 12 CowBoy Luis, Redreg, 2008. http://commons.wikimedia.org/wiki/ File:Cowboy-luis-redreg-allpsg.jpg Ⓢ

- p. 20 Two drawings of the "Scenes of Hazing", as printed in the 1880 Massachusetts Agricultural College yearbook. circa 1879. http://commons. wikimedia.org/wiki/File:EarlyMACHazing.png Ⓢ

- p. 26 Steel engraving by J. L. Raab, 1791 after a painting by Döbler. http:// commons.wikimedia.org/wiki/File:Immanuel_Kant_%28portrait%29.jpg

- p. 38 A portrait engraved for a posthumous edition of Rousseau's works, after an original by Angelique Briceau. http://commons.wikimedia.org/wiki/ File:Rousseau_in_later_life.jpg

- p. 44 Artwork by E. Burne-Jones, April 1888, for the first book edition of William Morris' A Dream of John Ball. Illustrates the couplet "When Adam delved and Eve span / Who was then the gentleman?" which had international popularity in several Germanic languages as an equalitarian slogan during the medieval period. http://commons.wikimedia.org/wiki/File:William.Morris. John.Ball.trimmed.jpg

- p. 48 Ecureuil espagnol Stencil of a shopping cart with the head of the consumer in the cart. An image from the spanish subvertising group Consume-HastaMorir, www.consumehastamorir.org May 2008. ①

- p. 56 Carlos Lugo, by Pteddy 16 December 2008. Ⓢ

- p. 61 Dennis Jarvis from Halifax, Canada. Reconstruction from the skull. Fossil of the skull of Lantian Man. The Paleolithic Age (about 1,150,000 years ago) excavated from Gongwangling, Lantian County. http://commons. wikimedia.org/wiki/File:Flickr_-_archer10_%28Dennis%29_-_DSC-N7342BB.jpg ⊚ ⊙

- p. 68 Bathurst Island men. Personal photographs of the Hon. C L A Abbott during his term as Administrator of the Northern Territory – Aborigine Chief of Bathurst Island who died of fright in Darwin when he saw his first motor car Date: 1939. http://commons.wikimedia.org/wiki/File:Bathurst_Island_men.jpg

- p. 74 Anti-Authoritarians Anonymous – Adventures in Subversion: Flyers and Posters, 1981-85 (San Francisco: Oh! Press, 1985) p. 12. No Copyright. http://radicalarchives.org/2012/10/03/aaa-adventures-in-subversion/

- p. 78 Português: Viagens de Gulliver, Parte III, Capítulo II http://commons. wikimedia.org/wiki/File:Viagens_de_Gulliver_054.jpg

- p. 86 Young Wild West and Silver Stream, or The White Girl Captive of the Sioux. By an Old Scout. Cover of Wild West magazine no. 284, 27 March 1908. http://commons.wikimedia.org/wiki/File:Wild_West_1908.jpg

- p. 92 Sitting Bull and Buffalo Bill, Montreal, QC, 1885 CALL NUMBER: LOT 12887 [item] [P&P] REPRODUCTION NUMBER: LC-USZ62-21207 (b&w film copy neg.) Photographer: David F. Barry MEDIUM: 1 photographic print . SUBJECTS: Buffalo Bill, 1846-1917. Sitting Bull, 1834?-1890. FORMAT: Portrait photographs 1890-1900. Group portraits 1890-1900. Photographic prints 1890-1900. REPOSITORY: Library of Congress Prints and Photographs Division Washington, D.C. 20540 USA DIGITAL ID: (digital file from b&w film copy neg.) cph 3a22279 http:// hdl.loc.gov/loc.pnp/cph.3a22279 CARD #: 2007675831. http://commons. wikimedia.org/wiki/File:Sitting_bull_and_buffalo_bill_c1885.jpg